Sandy Faulkner

WHOLLY GOD

The Story of a **Perfect God** and His **Peculiar People**

LEAFWOOD
PUBLISHERS

Abilene, Texas

WHOLLY GOD

The Story of a Perfect God and His Peculiar People

Copyright 2008 by Sandy Faulkner

ISBN 978-0-89112-572-3

Printed in the United States of America

Scripture quotations, unless otherwise noted, are from the Holy Bible, New International
Version® NIV® Copyright © 1973, 1978, 1984 by International Bible Society. Used by
permission of Zondervan Publishing House. All rights reserved. Scripture quotations marked
(kjv) are taken from the King James Version. Scripture quotations marked (Phillips) are
taken from The New Testament in Modern English, Revised Edition © 1972 by J. B. Phillips.
Copyright renewed © 1986, 1988 by Vera M. Phillips.

Italics in the Scripture quotations are the author's added emphasis.

Cover design by Greg Jackson, Thinkpen Design LLC

Interior text design by Sandy Armstrong

For information contact:
Leafwood Publishers, Abilene, Texas
1-877-816-4455 toll free
www.leafwoodpublishers.com

08 09 10 11 12 / 7 6 5 4 3 2 1

To Mikel Faulkner,
a wonderful husband
who has always believed in me.

ACKNOWLEDGEMENTS

Many thanks to the people at Leafwood Publishers who gave me the chance to live the dream of a published book:

Lisa Dickison who chose to believe in my somewhat off-kilter take on things biblical. Though it is common for everyone to think they have a book in them, she believed I actually did, and I am very grateful.

Dr. Leonard Allen who accompanied me on my journey through publishing, let me haggle over nuances and details I deemed crucial, and worked way too hard getting everything in the "go" position for this book. I appreciate him giving this book so much personal attention and time. It made all the difference.

Greg Taylor, the excellent editor who removed my excess verbiage and smoothed out the rough spots; Sandy Armstrong, the designer who gave the book its professional look; and Greg Jackson, the cover designer whose choice of lettering and fondness for camels gave the book a whimsical touch that felt like me.

Others who helped bring this book to fruition:

Carol Bartley, pre-publication editor. Her eye for detail is matched by her heart for God. The hours I spent across the table from her while she whittled away the excess and asked for more from me at the same time were some of the greatest hours I have ever spent. Knowing her better has enriched me. She is an excellent editor and a godly woman, whom I now count as a good friend.

My students. Thanks to all the students who have sat in my classroom through the years while I refined my life's work with the help of their feedback. Fifth graders and their parents and dozens of co-teachers through the decades have helped shape this book. My friends and the women from my Tuesday classes, who always wanted to "go back" to the fifth grade on Sunday morning to hear the lessons I taught there, encouraged me to fulfill this dream.

Mikel Faulkner. This is more than an acknowledgment; it is a dedication of this book to him. He is a wonderful husband and the best man I know. Almost single-handedly he made this book happen because he believed so deeply in me and insisted that others believe as well. He makes me want to be a better woman, and I thank God every day for being his wife.

Sandy Faulkner
July 2008

CONTENTS

PREFACE

EVERYTHING I NEED TO KNOW ABOUT GOD I LEARNED IN FIFTH GRADE

We all come to knowledge of God in our own way. I don't know what refined your faith in who God is and exactly what part He plays in your life, but I can tell you when certain things about God crystallized in my mind and heart. It was when I went back to the fifth grade.

For years right after college, I taught Sunday school to intermediate-age children. At some point I began to think, *I am too profound for children!* So I moved up and taught junior high, then high school, and finally adults, where my profundity could be fully appreciated. Before long I realized, *I am too simple for adults!* I found that the more complicated people's lives become, the more complicated they expect a message to be. We adults want Bible study to be advanced to appeal to our advanced spiritual development. We've been conditioned to believe that if the message is complicated, if it's beyond our comprehension, if it exceeds our grasp in any way, then it must be good or smart or spiritual.

Yet, in 1 Corinthians 1:21, Paul said, "God . . . in his wisdom chose to save all who would believe by the *'simple-mindedness'* of the gospel message" (Phillips). As I decided to return to teaching my first children's class in several years and began developing a curriculum, I realized something important: God's message is simply profound yet profoundly simple.

God's message is simply profound yet profoundly simple.

When I went back to the fifth grade, I went with a task: to teach students the *message* of the Old Testament. I also went with an agenda: to teach them more than I knew at their age, to teach them certain changeless principles they would need to trust as they grew spiritually. Every year they come to me knowing isolated facts about people and events in the Bible. In fact, I am frequently amazed by how many facts they do know. But I want them to know more than facts. I want them to meet God in the pages of the Bible. I want them to realize what it means to be God's child. And I want them to know what God has done to make them His.

My years in the fifth grade have challenged and inspired me to do, I believe, some of the best teaching of my life because I have found myself totally swept up in the very heart of the message I teach. I have been in Sunday school since birth. I have fifteen hours of Bible credit from a Christian university. I have been exposed to great preachers, teachers, and writers. But I only grasped the magnitude—the depth and width and height—of God's love and God's Word and God's plan when I had to simplify His message so children could understand it.

I need to tell you up front that I am not a scholar, nor is this a scholarly work. There is a lot I don't know. I can't comprehend all of God's ways and all of His thoughts. But I have become certain of one thing in all my years of teaching about God to His little children. In His Book, God laid out His heart for us to see. And what I see is a heart that desires nothing more than my heart's response to Him. His heart longs for mine. That is what I know about God. And that is the story I want to tell.

1 How Firm a Foundation?

A Very Good Place to Start

This is what the Lord says—your Redeemer, the Holy One of Israel:
"I am the Lord your God, who teaches you what is best for you,
who directs you in the way you should go."

—Isaiah 48:17

I remember vividly the day it happened, when all my previous knowledge and experience were not enough to get me through my present trial. It was my junior year in high school, and I was in Algebra II, standing before the bar of judgment. All alone at the blackboard, intellectually naked in front of the class, I had an inadequate understanding of the principles and no foundation on which to construct a solution to the problem that loomed in front of me. Somewhere along the way I had missed it—the underpinning, the facts and precepts that form the basis of higher mathematics. I was totally and completely lost. I didn't know where to begin to find an answer. Even today I never feel more helpless or hopeless than when I can't comprehend something I desperately need to know.

In algebra and in life, solutions are sometimes elusive. In order to find answers, we have to know foundational principles. Remembering the pain of insufficiency, I want my Bible students—and, truth be known, myself as well—to feel the assurance that comes from a bedrock understanding of the most important subject in the world: God and His Word.

THE STORY

Anyone who begins a study in the Bible needs to have a rudimentary knowledge of its structure. The ordinary citizen can usually name a few books in the Bible. At least I hope the average person's knowledge is not as limited as the old television show *Family Feud* indicated. During the lightning round of one episode, the only book of the Bible other than Genesis that one family could name was "Moses." Okay, they get credit for naming a great man who was the human author of five books in the Bible, but unfortunately none of his books bears his name. However, that wasn't as eye opening as another family in their lightning round saying that the only woman in the Bible they could name besides Mary was Lady Godiva!

So recognizing that some people really are starting from ground zero, I always remind my students of a few facts before we get into the *old,* old story, where knowledge of God really begins, and I ask them to consider what these facts might mean for our study together. Since the Bible is composed of sixty-six books containing 31,102 verses written by fortyish men over approximately fifteen hundred years, how many stories would they guess the Bible tells? Answers range from hundreds to thousands before I tell them what I consider the first important fact: there is *one story* in the Bible.

And, furthermore, I believe there is one verse that tells the Bible's one story, one that stands out as a summary of the whole Bible. Every year almost immediately one of my fifth graders comes up with the verse: John 3:16. It is probably the Bible's best-known verse and may be the only one that actually comes to a child's mind when I ask for a verse, but even if that is the case, it still counts as the right answer. John 3:16 is more than a sign to hold up at a sporting event. It is a sign of a plan. "For God so loved the world that he gave his one and only Son, that whoever believes in him shall not perish but have eternal life." One story runs from the opening chapters of Genesis to the closing chapters of Revelation. One story unites every event and every character in the Bible. It is the story of God's loving redemption, His plan to save His children, and it will unfold throughout our study of the Old Testament.

There is one story in the Bible. . . . And one verse tells the Bible's one story.

Just as there are many books and many verses in the Bible, there are many people within its pages. Although Lady Godiva is not one of them, hundreds of other colorful characters play important, even crucial, roles in the Bible story. Their lives teach us much about how we should live or, in many cases, not live. But I confess that it took me most of the first half of my life to discover that these weren't just isolated characters living heroic lives to teach some specific virtue. Each individual and event recorded in the Bible is there for a purpose. Each individual story of each character is a part of the whole—the one story that is the Bible story. And in telling these characters' stories, God tells us His.

Assuredly, the facts in the Bible are important, because they give us a foundation on which to build. And the heroes of the Bible are great to study, because they give us a heritage

> *The Bible is the story of what God wants us to know so we can know Him.*

to claim. But the Bible is not just a book of facts, and it is not just a history book about heroes. The Bible is the story of what God wants us to know so we can know Him.

Wholly Holy, Holy

In order to know God, we need to know about God's nature—what He is like, who He is. We need to know about God's will—what He wants to accomplish for us and in us. We need to know about God's heart—what matters to Him. We all need to define God in such a way that He will *be God* to us.

There are numberless ways to ascribe to God the "God-ness" He deserves. But among the descriptions of our glorious God is a word that is not "one of" His characteristics. It *is* His character. God is *holy.* He is set apart, set above all other things by His holiness. He is apart from any impure thing. He is above any mundane thing. He is sacred, divine, perfect, complete. He is wholly holy.

And because He is holy, God is too high for us to comprehend. His glory is too brilliant for human eyes. We cannot—ever—reach that high. We cannot—ever—comprehend that much. So holy God determined to find a way to reach impure humanity. And from the point of God's holiness, we begin to build an unimaginable and altogether awesome picture of how God would reveal Himself to us and begin His work of redemption to save us.

Steeped in sinfulness as we are, adults have a hard time grasping the concept of holiness. How much more true for children. My first goal as a teacher of fifth graders was to translate my understanding of who God is into words children could understand and remember, and I wanted simple symbols to represent a complex concept. I came up with three immediately and had a fourth one pointed out by a friend who happened into my classroom halfway through my first year.

The first symbol I put on the board in every opening class represents the purity and rightness of God. It's the symbol for what God can't do: . A major part of God's holiness is that He cannot sin. It is against everything He is. God cannot be with sin. God cannot abide sin. In fact, God hates sin. This undeniable part of His character will help explain some of His actions as He deals with His children throughout the Bible.

The second symbol is . God is, in fact, the opposite of evil. Everything He is, is good. Everything He does is good. It is impossible for Him to be or do anything else. Everything He says is good. Everything He demands is good. Everything He allows is *for* good. Believing this, I must trust Him even when it seems His *definition* of good differs greatly from my own.

The third symbol is . This is my favorite part of God's nature, the part I want to claim for myself. It incorporates His mercy and the "amazingness" of His grace. Love is the grace giver, the mercy motivator. This symbol represents the *why* behind *what* God has done. His undeniable love for humanity, His overwhelming love for me, move Him to act on humanity's behalf, on my behalf. Creation, incarnation, salvation—all are acts of unfathomable love. Jesus said that all the Law is summed up in love. The apostle Paul, speaking with the guidance of God's Spirit, said that the greatest thing is love and that no action taken outside of love really matters. Love is God's reason, His motivation, for what He does. "For God so loved the world *that* he gave . . . "

> To save the people He loves from the sin He hates, God Himself would become the sacrifice for all the wrongs, and He would make it all right.

The fourth symbol is . If love is our favorite and the easiest one to accept, justice is the most frightening and the hardest to accept, at least for ourselves. This symbol of God's nature is at once edifying and terrifying. Justice is a pledge that things *must* and *will* be made right. This part of God not only hates sin but is pledged to punish it and the purveyors of it as well. Wrong must be righted by a righteous and just God.

But here is where the hard part gets good. We find out that the God who hates sin also loves people. So to save the people He loves from the sin He hates, God Himself would become the sacrifice for all the wrongs, and He would make it all right. That's His justice.

WHY WHO?

Why is it important to know certain unassailable facets of God's nature as we begin to tell His story? Because we don't get far into studying the Bible before we read some pretty horrifying stories, stories where on the surface God seems neither good or loving. There are tough stories where the whole world is wiped out by a flood; where an entire family is swallowed up apparently to punish one man's sin; where a man is struck dead for just touching something; where a city is razed and all its inhabitants, including women, children, and even animals, are killed; where rebellious children are ordered to be stoned; and where a woman was "pillar-ed" for looking back at what she might be missing.

When you can't understand the what or the why, trust the Who. Believe in the God you know.

What do we do with a God like that if we don't know Him? What do we do when we face our own horrifying experiences? What do we do when someone we need dies? What if a loved one leaves? What about financial hardship, illness, accidents, prejudice, unkindness, unfairness? What do we do with a God who allows those things if we don't already know Him? Nonbelievers, and even doubting believers, rationalize their lack of faith by the question "What kind of a God would (fill in the blank) ?" Our survival of that question lies in our knowledge of and our faith in who God is.

I want my students to always refer back to those symbols of who God is as we discuss difficult things in His Word. And I want to always go back to who He is when I experience difficult things in my life. Because of who God is—because He is all good, because His motivation is always love, because it is impossible for Him to do anything wrong, because He can and will make all things right—He is a God who can always be trusted by those who know Him. Someone once said, "When you can't trace His hand, trust His heart." When you can't understand the *what* or the *why*, trust the *Who.* Believe in the God you know.

2 O What a Beautiful Morning

Creation

For since the creation of the world
God's invisible qualities—his eternal power and divine nature—
have been clearly seen.

—Romans 1:20

GENESIS 1–2

My dad grew up in the deep woods of East Texas, and I mean *deep* woods. He came from a family who struggled economically, physically, and probably even psychically. If my father hadn't been a really good basketball player, I might be sitting right now in a copse of trees with a shotgun, trying to protect the family moonshine from poachers and revenuers. But because he could dribble and shoot, my dad became the first person in his family to get out of the woods and the only one to go to college. That made most of the difference in his life . . . and most likely mine.

There are people in our country who can track their personal histories all the way back to royalty or to historically significant relatives. Others have come from financially influential or academically important families. But most people have pretty humble beginnings and some, even ignominious ones. Obviously I can't trace my physical bloodline to any origin resembling glorious, but my lifeline? That's a different matter. It began in glory. It began in the beginning. Its origin was with God.

"In the beginning God . . . " Those words say it all. What existed in the beginning? God existed. What is God's origin? Try to wrap your finite mind around the fact that the Originator had no origin. He just *is*. I think that is why God's introduction of Himself to Israel through Moses has such an impact on me. He said simply, "I AM." That explains everything. He *is*. And I am because He is. Life is because He is. All things began because He, the One who exists, began them. My brain cannot begin to comprehend how it all happened, but my heart swells at the contemplation of why it happened.

Why? Is there a deeper question in the universe than the one that begins with "why"? What parent, what teacher does not dread the question that begins that way? "What" is factual. "How" is demonstrable. "Where" is definable. But "why" is sometimes inexplicable. "Why" often cannot be truly answered and frequently will not be explored. I don't want to search too deeply into the shady recesses of why I do some of the things I do. It exposes too clearly what lies beneath the veneer of Christianity that I present to the world. It reveals too much of who I really am inside. It has to do with *heart*.

> *At the heart of the question of why God created is, I believe, the heart of God.*

Doesn't everything? How much more could God have emphasized the value He puts on the content of the heart? At the heart of the question "why?" is the heart. And at the heart of the question of why God created is, I believe, the heart of God.

LOVE DIVINE, ALL LOVE EXCELLING

God never tells us why He began to create, but I believe the answer to "why" lies in "who." I remind my students of how we described God. What is His character? It is holiness. It is the absence of any sin, the presence of absolute goodness, the unfailing ability to make things right, and it is all motivated by love. I believe that God's motive for everything He does—His why—is His abiding love. So why did God create? Simply put, I believe He created mankind to love, and to love Him in return. Before God even created humans, He was moved by love for us. All that exists was created for the creature God chose to love. Oh the things He did for love!

God has done many wondrous things—too many to count, too wondrous to grasp. But sometimes He seems to outdo Himself. Sometimes His love is so astounding that it knocks us to our knees when we truly see it. In the midst of God's countless acts of love, I believe Scripture gives us three especially great revelations of overwhelming love.

Bypassing the first one for a moment, I believe the second act of unfathomable love to be His *incarnation*. God the Son left glory and all that it signifies when He entered our world. What unbearable pain must He have endured in leaving the world of the spirit to become flesh and to live among people as the Son of Man. But He came and He lived so we might witness firsthand His love for us.

The third act of inconceivable love was *salvation*. The flawless and innocent Lamb of God offered His incarnated flesh as a sacrifice for sin. He sacrificed Himself so we might *believe* His love for us, and He rose that we might *receive* His love forever.

> *He put into action a plan we can't comprehend, to deliver us from a fate we can't imagine, for a reason we can't fathom.*

Two acts of overwhelming love—incarnation and salvation. And the first act of indescribable love? *Creation.* He began it all so we could live and move and have our being in Him. And when we failed Him, He put into action a plan we can't comprehend, to deliver us from a fate we can't imagine, for a reason we can't fathom.

The things He does for love!

And so it began . . .

IMAGINE THAT!

"In the beginning God created the heavens and the earth." Even in the word *create* is God's essence. It means "to bring into being," "to cause to exist." The world simply wouldn't be if it hadn't been created. It wasn't manufactured from existing parts. It didn't evolve from something else. Something came from nothing because of God. "Now the earth was formless and empty, darkness was over the surface of the deep." Formless, empty, dark, deep: a description of the nothingness that existed before God created. "And the Spirit of God was hovering over the waters." God looked down on nothing, but like an expectant and protective parent, He prepared for the coming of something spectacular.

Dare we believe creation was routine for God? The words in Scripture sound so unadorned that we may miss the passion the Creator must have felt as He brought something from nothing. This was all brand-new! The celestial beings must have watched in awe as God began to unfold His plan. They saw the nothing that existed, but God's eternal eyes saw what He wanted to make and why He wanted to make it. He had a purpose only He could fathom. He would make something beautiful, something wondrous, a world that when seen and experienced would evoke absolute awe in those who were created to live in it. The created could look at the creation and know that the Creator *is*. "The heavens declare the glory of God . . . [and] proclaim the work of his hands." "For since the creation of the world, God's invisible qualities—his eternal power and divine nature—have been clearly seen, being understood from what has been made, so that men are without excuse." With only a word from the depths of His heart, God spoke into being all that exists. And what wonder He created!

Dare we believe creation was routine for God?

LIGHTS! ACTION!

The Creator looked down on nothing—that empty formlessness covered in darkness. Then with His powerful finger, He stirred the nothingness and spoke into the darkness: "Let there be light." And at His word, the light of the Lord God dispelled and displaced the all-pervasive darkness. With light God declared, "I AM." Since the beginning, light has declared the presence of God.

Following the announcement of His presence to the world, the Almighty proclaimed His power. At His mere utterance, an inhabitable world began to form. The Creator created atmosphere—warmth, moisture, gravity, a perfect blend of gases for breathing. He designed climates and made weather. He stored up rain and snow, wind and lightning, castles of clouds, searing heat.

The next step by the divine Architect and Engineer was to give form to the formless. He shaped land. He separated the waters, making the oceans and seas both boundless and bound. The tide never stops, never sleeps. Yet God "fixed limits for it and set its doors and bars in place" and told it, "This far you may come and no farther; here is where your proud waves halt." In the midst of the waters covering the planet's surface, God made giant continents and tiny islands. He put salt into the sea for cleansing and fresh water on the land for nourishing. What jubilance the Creator must have felt as He scooped out valleys and molded mountains. I imagine that He planned as He shaped: Here on this mountain I will give my Law! That valley is where I shall win a victory for my army! What joy it must have been to carve rivers and etch streams, build waterfalls and dig underground springs. The Lord God made a beautiful framework for His world. That which had been formless now had magnificent form.

Land and Sea and Sky ... Oh My!

After giving form to the formless, God began to fill what had been empty. The land was covered with things that would grow. He made trees. And the grand Designer didn't just make *a* tree. He made giant redwoods, some large enough to drive a car through. He made snazzy palms for postcards from your vacation in paradise, graceful willows for lazy days of reading, sturdy oaks for climbing and swinging. He tailored shapely and aromatic pines to stand beside the fireplace at Christmas, to wear gaudy baubles and fill the room with the fragrance of holiday. He made trees that grow fruit—and not just the apple-a-day-that-keeps-the-doctor-away kind of fruit, but juicy peaches, fragrant oranges, exotic mangoes and papayas. He made berries for cobblers, and He made vegetables for vitamins.

The Divine Florist also arranged flowers by the millions. Sweet-smelling roses for anniversaries and New Year's Day floats. Mysterious orchids that grow only in expensive greenhouses carefully tended by experts or that grow wild in the jungle carefully hidden from the prying of "experts." He shaped daisies for testing the veracity of love and made daffodils to herald the arrival of spring. He created flowers that specialize in seasons where others wither: mums for fall, pansies for winter. He made plants that amaze: cacti that thrive without water, bromeliads that grow on rocks. He formed leaves of all shapes and sizes: leaves the size of a hair and, in the tropics, leaves the size of a car door! He made leaves so diverse that science projects might look impressive. That day just had to be blooming beautiful!

It must have also been the day the Lord made the first nature sounds to soothe us on our relaxation CDs—babbling water, whispering foliage. It definitely had to be the day that He painted with the abundant colors we love! Teal, azure, turquoise for water. Chartreuse, vermilion, saffron for leaves. A veritable and vivid polychrome of flowers.

Even in the unseen areas of His world, God made exquisite surprises for those who would search. Sparkling gemstones—bright shining diamonds, deep green emeralds, rich red rubies, beautiful blue sapphires—hidden inside ugly rocks.

God had formed the formless, and He had begun to fill the empty. With great style He had accomplished it, and with breathtaking beauty He had enriched it! And when the Maker finished that day's work, He looked at what He had done, and He must have said with great satisfaction, "Now that is good."

But He had only begun. His next project was to decorate the skies—that part of His creation that would most visibly shout the name "Creator." On this day the Almighty gathered His light into bodies that would either shine light or reflect it for all to see.

Our sun was designed for warmth and for time, for seasons and for growth, and for hope that another day will follow. (Ask any singing orphan. They can assure you that the sun will come out tomorrow!) All day every day the sun proclaims the power and presence of its Creator.

And when the sun disappears beneath the horizon at nightfall, there is still assurance of its presence and no loss of hope, because our moon calmly reflects back to us the light of the day just past and illuminates the night ahead. The moon is a quiet reminder that light is present even in a darkened world and there is hope of more to come. More mysterious than the blatant power of the sun is the moon's peaceful vigil. Yet it moves our oceans, motivates our lovers, and summons our scientists and dreamers alike.

The moon is a quiet reminder that light is present even in a darkened world and there is hope of more to come.

Then there are the stars and outer space, which may be the most alluring testimony of all. God flung into the darkness handfuls of light. Stars to guide the ancient mariners. Stars to wish upon. Stars to urge the mind to "boldly go where no man has gone before." What a challenge to the mind of man. We have been told that space grows at the rate of 1,500 miles a day. How could that be? How can the human mind even conceive of such vastness? How could it be that traveling at the speed of light—186,000 miles per second!—in 10,000 years one would be only halfway through *our* galaxy? And our galaxy is one of, well, who knows how many galaxies? What absolute wonder fills my heart and what amazement fills my tiny brain as I try to fathom a small portion of the information we *know*. How big is our God? Try to explain it or define it or describe it. I can't. My only response is total awe. No wonder the psalmist proclaimed that the heavens themselves shout the name of their Creator for all to see. Joseph Addison, in the hymn "The Spacious Firmament on High," depicts the glory in beautiful poetry:

> The unwearied sun, from day to day, does his Creator's powers display
> And publishes to every land the work of an Almighty Hand.
> Soon as the evening shades prevail, the moon takes up the wondrous tale
>
> And nightly to the listening earth repeats the story of her birth;
> While all the stars that round her burn, and all the planets in their turn,
> Confirm the tidings as they roll, and spread the truth from pole to pole. . . .
> In reason's ear they all rejoice and utter forth a glorious voice,
> Forever singing as they shine, "The hand that made us is divine."

Nowhere is God more evident than in the heavens. Surely hope filled His heart that day as He beckoned all beings to behold His greatness, His vastness, His infinite power visible to those who would search the heavens and see the God who created them. And He has let us know what He thought of His work that day. In what seems like a gross under-statement when we consider the magnitude of the message, God declared it a *good* day.

After covering the heavens with celestial bodies that herald His majesty, God turned His imagination toward the beings that would occupy the space above and beneath the surface of the earth. If you stop and consider just the *order* of creation, you see the mind of God working. Already He had made atmosphere, water, and land. He had created warmth and light to sustain the plants, which He had made to sustain the animals, which He had yet to create. Creation was masterfully planned and executed. With such a heart and such a mind had God designed and constructed. And with such style did He fill what He had formed.

The Creator filled the skies with imaginative creatures. Tiny finches and huge condors. Fluttering hummingbirds and soaring eagles. Minute to majestic and every-thing in between. Birds that sing a beautiful song. Birds that herald the day. Birds that just squawk. Birds that will carry messages. Birds that fly home to nest, even if home is thousands of miles away from where they live in the off-season. Birds that look like flying flowers. Birds with faces only a mother could love. Toucans, cardinals, dodos. What greater variety could there be?

How about the variety He put in the water! Into ponds and rivers, into the deep recesses of the oceans, into the vast expanses of water that covered the surface of the earth, God poured perhaps the most diverse creatures of all. Fish of every color from camouflaged can't-spot-me-if-you-try gray to can't-miss-me neon yellow and blue. From super slick to scary spiny. Long-tailed stingrays. Many-legged octopuses. Many-teethed sharks. Creatures that can be viewed only through a scuba mask or on a National Geographic special. Creatures seen exclusively at submarine depth by special cameras and still others that scientists suspect have never been seen. Millions of *types* of water dwellers. Why so many? Why so varied? Why did God make such amazing things that have to be sought in order to be seen? Why did He put air-breathing animals in the water? Was it so they would be forced to the surface where we could see them and marvel at the God who made them?

It thrills my soul to imagine what must have been in the heart of God as He created the fantastic beings that inhabit the air and the water. With what satisfaction must He have announced that day of creation—a roaring success to my way of thinking—was, like the ones that preceded it, *good.*

The Ape Was Great

As God began His final day of creation, do you suppose the angels wondered what He could possibly do to top what He had already done? Could life be any more beautiful than that which inhabits the skies or more intriguing than that which dwells in the sea? How the watchers must have gaped as the Creator began producing the animals that would live on the surface of the perfectly prepared planet. On the final day God went wild . . . wild kingdom to be exact! He painted stripes on tigers and zebras, dots on leopards. He stretched out the giraffe's neck and the elephant's nose. He put a house on a turtle's back and a horn on a rhino's face. He made animals that would become companions to lounge in your lap while you watch TV, and He made animals that would work hard for a living. He made animals that would give us food and animals that would become our food. He made animals that crawl, animals that climb, animals that hop, animals that swing by their tails, animals that walk, very slowly, upside down in trees, and He made a cat that can outrun a sports car. He dreamed up bees and spiders and insects for nature magazines and Discovery Channel specials. He made animals that would confound the world's scientists. A duckbilled platypus—is it an amphibian or a mammal? Turns out it's a mammal, but it has webbed feet and a bill, and it lays eggs! Mammals don't do that! Do they?

It appears the Lord had a blast that day thinking up quirky, exotic, and beautiful living things. And He appears to have put them into a benign world where the other living things that inhabited their space were not interested in consuming them. Genesis 1:30 seems to declare a vegetarian existence for all creatures on the land. The creation was a place of beauty and a place of serene, ordered peace. And it was *good.*

But Man Was the Plan

From the imagination of an infinite God had come the creation of this world. From darkness God had brought light. From formlessness God had created structure. What had been a void God had filled. No longer dark, no longer formless, no longer empty, the world was fully prepared to receive what it had all been *for.* Only then, with everything ready, everything intricately designed and flawlessly executed, did God set Himself to the task planned from the beginning.

Did He seem different to those beings watching in the heavenly realms? Did an expectant hush fall across heaven as the Lord of the universe gathered Himself for the mission ahead? I wonder if the angels held their breath as they saw Him reach toward the earth He had created. So much was at stake now. This was what the entire creative process had all been about. This was the reason for all He'd done to this point. This was it. The crown of the creation.

God reached down into the soil of His perfect creation and gently scooped up some clay. Tenderly, with His own hands, He formed His very special creature. Not with His booming voice did the Almighty speak mankind into existence, but with His loving hands He molded. And in the grasp of God, humanity took shape. Every organ, every limb, every tiny hair that covered man's body was shaped by the hands of the Father. Every cell, every enzyme, every trace element was overseen. Nothing was accidentally or unnecessarily added. Nothing was carelessly left out. A perfect being

Soul deep, we are God's Divine DNA.

emerged, designed by the mind of God, formed by the hands of God. We were handmade by God. How could it be that we matter so much to Him! To authenticate the value of what He had made, He stamped on mankind the sign of His divine approval: "Made in the image of God." Soul deep, we are God's Divine DNA.

Tenderly cradling the creature He had molded, God gently breathed into him the breath of life, the eternal spirit that would inhabit his body. And man became a living being.

In the scriptural rendering it sounds so routine, this bestowing of life. How ungrateful and shortsighted we would be to consider it so. In a momentary breath God gave us His most precious gift. In His hands alone is life. Science has tried to explain it, but can't. Scientists have tried to create it, but won't. Oh, they'll continue, because in the arrogance that is so typical of humankind, man tends to believe that the secret of his life lies somewhere within himself. Experimentation has cloned a sheep from existing materials, and those who experiment have predicted that the actual creation of life is close at hand in their laboratories. From the fiction of Frankenstein to the science fiction of Dolly the sheep, mankind has taken God's gift of life and tried to usurp His position in bestowing it. It won't happen. "He himself gives all men life and breath and everything else." When God breathed His own life into His creature, He confirmed His love and clinched His ownership of man's soul forever. It was more than life that God breathed into mankind on that day. It was *eternal life*. It was the chance to live with God. God made the world for man, and God made man for Himself, forever.

As the final day of God's work in creation ended, He looked at all He had done and this time pronounced it *very* good. "Very good." Again, does that seem like just

> *God made the world for man, and God made man for Himself, forever.*

the tiniest understatement when your eyes behold the grandeur of this earth, when your mind struggles with the vastness of this universe, when your heart responds to the undeniable evidence of the divine Source of all you are? But when "good" sufficed for the spectacular creation that preceded the advent of mankind, then "very good" is a ringing endorsement of just how much God loved what He did when He completed creation in us!

In the midst of all the good He did on the closing day, God took time to survey and see that only one thing was *not* good. The man God had made needed a special companion to make him complete. So God, in fulfilling all the components of "very good," made woman. And there you have it. Woman: the completion of perfection!

God's in His Heaven, and All's Right with the World

God took His new creatures, Adam and Eve, and placed them in the perfect world He had created just for them. He set them in the garden and put them in charge of His creation with the admonition to care about it and care for it. Rule. Subdue. Fill the earth with offspring. Be good stewards of all that God has given.

Then God rested from all His work, and He blessed the seventh day and made it holy. He had completed His task. He had accomplished perfection in six days of labor, and the Lord was satisfied with the outcome. It was a day to glory in what He had done, to take His ease in the excellence of His world. The day would, in the future, become a day for people to rest from their work as well and, like the Father, glory in all that God has done on our behalf.

What a wondrous view of peaceful perfection. Genesis 2 closes with perfect creatures inhabiting a perfect creation with the Perfect Creator as a constant companion and guide. Everything looked, smelled, sounded, and tasted perfect. Everything worked perfectly.

What more could mankind possibly desire than perfection itself?

But what good is perfection when man's *desire* is involved?

3 It All Comes Tumbling Down

The Fall of Man

Sin is crouching at your door; it desires to have you.

—Genesis 4:7

GENESIS 3

Is it ever okay to wonder what God might be thinking? I'm absolutely certain it's not a good idea to question whether He knows what He's doing. But haven't you wondered what moved God to make some of His decisions regarding human beings? For instance, does it seem like a completely good idea to make a perfect world and then leave it under the jurisdiction of the average human?

I shouldn't ever be left in charge of anything. I hardly manage myself. My two children barely escaped childhood alive because I was the one looking after them. When I remember some of the things I did or didn't do as a mother of young children, it frightens me to realize just how often they probably evaded disaster because I was distracted or deluded or even bordered on demented. My eminently sensible and freakishly organized husband worked long hours and traveled in his job for a large company when our children were young. The poor innocents were left in the primary care of a true novice who was neither sensible nor organized. I learned intercessory prayer for my children when I recognized just how incompetent I was at parenting, and I learned "arrow" prayers as I frequently thanked the Lord for routinely sparing my children from (still another of) my inabilities. My son and daughter love me, but

I'm pretty sure they would blanch if they thought I was in charge of anything much bigger than a family meal. I know they would demand a recount if I was ever elected to manage the world.

However, Almighty God placed great trust in the hand of mankind. In spite of my thoughts on the matter, the perfect God, with His perfect reason, put His perfect creature in charge of His perfect creation.

What would happen to perfection?

THE CHOICE

In the middle of the story of God's creation of man, in Genesis 2, comes a seemingly innocuous comment. Verse 8 sets the scene: "Now the Lord God had planted a garden in the east, in Eden; and there he put the man he had formed." Then verse 9 is gently laid out: "And the Lord God made all kinds of trees grow out of the ground—trees that were pleasing to the eye and good for food. In the middle of the garden were the tree of life and the tree of the knowledge of good and evil." God seems to have said, "In my garden are all kinds of trees *just for you!* Trees for eyes to enjoy seeing, trees with fruit for bodies to enjoy consuming—all kinds of trees for you! And there are a couple of other trees as well . . . " In the midst of telling us about the trees in the garden and the rivers that watered the garden, God tells us the names of the rivers and the names of *just* a couple of trees. I have a little suggestion whenever you're reading God's Word: never assume anything is "just . . . "

Soon after that innocent verse comes this follow-up in verses 16–17: "And the LORD God commanded the man, 'You are free to eat from any tree in the garden; but you must not eat from the tree of the knowledge of good and evil, for when you eat of it you will surely die.'" Despite my having read that verse to my fifth graders many times over the years, the word "commanded" jumped out at me for the first time in a recent reading. Its emphasis seemed glaring, so I went back and reread the first two chapters of Genesis and found something I hadn't noticed before. In the text that precedes this verse, there is no reference to God "commanding" anything. From the first instance of God expressing Himself, when He spoke things into existence, the word "said" is used. God *said*, "Let there be light." God *said*, "Let there be an expanse between the waters . . . let there be lights in the expanse . . . let the water teem with living creatures . . . let birds fly above . . . let the land produce . . . let us make man in our image." God *said,* "Be fruitful and increase in number."

Those are pretty potent things that God simply *said.* He spoke a perfect world into existence by just *saying,* "Let it be." He gave His first marching orders to man by *saying,* "Take care of this world I made for you." I have always imagined God shouting to pierce the darkness when He called out, "Let there be light!" But there isn't an exclamation point in the NIV. He may have used His still, small voice. He could have whispered. He didn't need to shout. He has that much authority. What an exhibition of power to simply speak this magnificent world into being.

However, when we get to Genesis 2:16, God *commanded* Adam to listen up to what was coming. Is commanding just for laying down the law? If so, we should listen carefully and be aware of how important it is, both to God and to us, when He commands anything. God seemed to say, "Hear me, my child. This is of monumental importance for your well-being!" And then He proceeded to give Adam a command with eternal implications: "You are free to eat from any tree in the garden, but you must not eat from the tree of the knowledge of good and evil, for when you eat of it you will surely die."

It's interesting how many patterns are repeated in the Scriptures. God recognizes human inability to get it the first time, so He patiently tells us certain things over and over, hoping we'll eventually grasp both what He is saying and that He means what He is saying. As God tells Adam about the trees, we see the start of one of those patterns: God frequently lays out promises and warnings together. He tells His people what He wants to do for them and where He wants to lead them, and at the same time He warns them what will happen if they don't follow Him. God told the people they had an abundance of freedom: "You are free to eat from any tree . . . " Remember, He had made "all kinds of trees . . . trees that were pleasing . . . and good." The Father reminded the children of all He had provided just for them, and they were free to eat from the trees, apparently even the tree of life. Only one tree in the entire garden was withheld from them. Everything given by God was given in love and given for good. (Remember the symbols of His nature?) Could it be that one thing was withheld for the same reason?

God frequently lays out promises and warnings together.

Note the contrast between the two trees that are named, between what is offered and what is withheld. Now ponder the difference. Whenever I get to this point in the study with my fifth graders, I place on the board pictures of two trees. One is labeled "Life" and is covered with fruit. The other is labeled "Knowledge of Good and Evil" and is covered with sparkles and shiny trinkets. I then talk about what God offers to His children and the choice He allows us to make. He tells us we may choose life with the Giver of good things: stability, security, safety . . . life inside God's world. The other choice people can make is for different, new, exciting—"more" than what God offers, a life outside the boundaries. In other words, God gives us the choice of what *He offers* or what *we want*. He offers us everything "except . . . "

What is it with humans and the forbidden fruit? Why does the word *except* hang out there in front of our eyes, tempting us to grab it? Why can't we be content with what is good for us and not yearn for that which is likely to destroy us? Why isn't jogging as attractive as watching television and broccoli as appealing as chocolate? Since God knew (He *is* omniscient!) that we would more often than not choose incorrectly, why did He give us the freedom of choice, especially since the consequences of our wrong choices will destroy all He wants for us? He commanded in Genesis 2:17, "You must not eat from the tree of the knowledge of good and evil, for *when* you eat of it you will surely die." The Lord knew man would sin. Yet He gave us the choice to obey . . . or disobey.

Why?

A REALLY HEART CHOICE

Every year, I get the same question from a ten-year-old and often my co-teachers as well: "Why?" I am then forced to admit I don't actually know all the answers. All I have to build any answer upon is the certainty of what I know about God. I believe God's motivation for what He does is love. Love is the *why* in the *who* of God. "For God so loved that he gave . . . " His overwhelming love for humanity is what moves Him to act. God chose us. He chose to love us.

> *Love is the why in the who of God.*

Love is a choice we make as well. God wants to know if we will *choose* Him. The word is huge. Our choices come from deep inside, from what we value. So a choice to love is a heart response. As we progress through the study of God's plan in God's Word, we will see just how much

God values the heart. The "man after [God's] own heart" will demonstrate that. The New Testament writings are filled with the importance of heart. Much of God's revelation is about His heart, and much is made in His revelation about *my* heart. If God's heart response toward me is to choose to love me, what must I believe He wants in return? Could the Lord want any less than for me to choose to believe Him, choose to glorify Him, choose to obey Him because I have chosen to love Him? Where is my heart? What will I choose? Where will it lead?

> *If God's heart response toward me is to choose to love me, what must I believe He wants in return?*

There are very few words in God's first command to mankind, but the implications are huge: to obey or disobey, to believe or disbelieve, to love or withhold love, to honor God's desire or to go one's own way. Upon mankind's choice hangs the balance of the entire relationship between man and God. It can't get bigger than that. Man chooses the relationship, and everything else will follow his choice.

Bedeviled, Bothered, and Bewildered

I'd really like to know how much time passed between God's placing of Adam and Eve in the garden with a choice of trees on which to nosh and Eve's standing before *the* tree. We know from the Genesis 5 genealogy only two things concerning the age of Adam. He was 930 years old when he died, and he was 130 when his son Seth was born outside the garden. Did the years in the garden count toward his final age, or did being designed to live forever in God's presence mean his aging didn't start until he went outside? Whichever is true, the life spans of Adam and Eve were considerable, and surely at least some time passed in the garden before the two went totally haywire. Perhaps Eve and Adam had plenty of time to think about the forbidden tree and God's warning. People just *wonder,* you know. Maybe enough time had passed in the garden that human nature was already yearning for something new, different, exciting. Maybe Adam and Eve had even briefly entertained the thought that they would like to have that special knowledge implied by the tree's name, to know the unknown. Maybe they were just curious about what the Almighty meant when He referred to death.

Whatever the reason, at some point while living in the midst of perfection, Adam and Eve became vulnerable. It seems logical to me that when Satan, in the guise of the beautiful serpent, led Eve to the tree for her fateful taste, it wasn't her first trip in that direction. Had she wandered past it while gathering fruit for dinner from one of the permissible trees? Had she glanced at it and wondered what made God so adamant about the tree? Had she occasionally lingered and gazed at the tree, speculating about its forbidden power?

Something about the particular moment must have convinced Satan the time was right to make his move on God's children. James 1:13–15 tells us that we are "tempted . . . by [our] own evil *desire.*" Desire: the tingling yearning for something, or just something *else* . . . the urge that drags away and entices . . . the inner longing that (note the feminine terminology and think of Eve) when it "has conceived, it gives birth to sin." And when the child, sin, is fully grown, it "gives birth to death." Eve's choice would affect every generation to follow. Did she know where it would lead? No. All she knew was that she desired. Eve's quest for "whatever" convinced her to try what Satan offered. And whatever convinced Satan to tempt Eve, we only know that one day in paradise God's blessed one met up with God's wicked and committed enemy, and the choice made that day would change the course of humanity forever.

No Know!

There is so much we don't know about Satan. I think God purposely gives only glimpses of His enemy in the Scriptures because He desires to protect us from the wiles of the wicked one, not expose us to him. God urges us to pursue knowledge of He who desires to save us and not seek knowledge of the one who fervently longs to bring us eternal harm.

Brief revelations of Satan and his work are given in the Old Testament books of Daniel and Job, and poetic renderings in Revelation speak of the cosmic war that has raged and continues to rage. But most of what we know about Satan's origin comes from Ezekiel 28:12–19 and Isaiah 14:12–15. *Satan* means "the adversary," someone who is *against* us. He goes by many names: the devil, the Evil One, the Prince of Darkness, Beelzebub, Abaddon ("the destroyer"), and Lucifer ("shining one" or "light-bearer," sometimes translated "bringer of light").

That last name, Lucifer, is the most chilling to me. "Fans" of Lucifer say that he represents the questioning mind, the independent thinker—things our society admires and might even care to emulate. When I study Satan with my fifth graders, I first have them draw a picture of what they believe he looks like and list words that describe him. After they show their renderings and we compile their list of descriptive words, I challenge their notions of how he would look if we could see him. If Satan appeared to us as scary and ugly and in all the hideous manifestations depicted by movies, television, and tales of the bogeyman, our instinct would be to flee from him as rapidly as possible. And that is why he doesn't appear that way. In order to defeat God, which is his goal, Satan has to win God's people. No one wins allegiance by frightening away the object of his desire. One wins by wooing, by luring, by enticing, by drawing to instead of driving away. Hence, Satan "masquerades as an angel of light," beautiful and alluring, offering us what we *want*, what we think we *need*, what we believe we *deserve*.

In order to defeat God, Satan has to win God's people.

Fallen Star

According to the accounts of Satan's origin, he is well-suited for the task of attracting people. He was an angel created by God. He was even an important and beautiful angel, maybe the most beautiful of them all. Ezekiel proclaims him as the "model of perfection, full of wisdom and perfect in beauty." He is described as one adorned in precious stones and purest gold. He was "anointed" and "ordained" by God. He was designated as a guardian cherub. We don't know for sure what Satan guarded (did he guard Eden, as some have surmised, or even the throne of God, as others have theorized?), but any guard has a position of trust. Satan was on the holy mount of God, where he "walked among" the holy things. He had access to God Most High. He *knew* God. In fact, he had it all until "wickedness was found" in him.

Satan's heart became proud because of his beauty (which God had created), and he was corrupted because he was so enamored of his splendor (which God had created). When he became so impressed with himself, Satan became preposterously ambitious. The created angel wanted to reign in the place of the One who had created him in the first place. It's a good thing human beings haven't ever entertained those kinds of ideas, isn't it! Satan declared himself an enemy of God when he decided he was going to take God's place. In his own mind he was equipped to lead the entire host of heaven. And he was at least impressive (or persuasive) enough to lead a large number of God's host into rebellion against Him. (How easy is it for mankind to resist such appeal?)

Satan has power all right. But he doesn't have enough to overcome God Most High, who has all power over all things. When he rebelled against God in heaven, Satan was banished from God's heavenly realm.

Here's the part that makes one's blood run cold: the place to which he was banished. When I tell my kids that Satan was kicked out of heaven, I ask them where he was kicked "to." They always say—without actually saying it, of course, because they are in Sunday school—that he was kicked down to hell. Oh that it were true! Hell has been prepared for the devil and his angels, and it is where he will be bound for eternity when the Lord wraps it all up, but until that time, according to Isaiah 14:12, Satan was cast down to *earth*. And here, on earth where mankind would live, the devil began to make himself at home.

FALLING FOR IT

So on that fateful day in the garden, perhaps because God's precious creature looked especially vulnerable or maybe just for the "hell" of it, Satan made a move on God's world again. And this time, as a result of Satan's actions, someone else would be banished from home.

Here is what we know about the devil in serpent's clothing that Eve met in the garden that day: he was by now quite at home in the outside world; he was adept at concealing ugliness behind a facade; he was a silver-tongued devil; he knew about the garden, the people, and the God who loved them; and he hated God for defeating him. If Satan wanted to get back at the God he hated with every fiber of his being, what was his best opportunity? He could get the people God loved with every fiber of His being. Satan could insert himself into the humans' lives. He could convince them their God was not who He claimed to be. He could separate them from their God. He could win them to his way. He could rule their decisions and their desires. It seemed a workable plan. So . . . one day Lucifer (evil disguised in beauty, darkness cloaked in light) sidled up to Eve with a *new* idea, *different* options, a *better* plan for her life. He gave her a good sales pitch: the possibility of tastier fruit than God's. And as we all know, Eve bit—on the sales pitch and then on the fruit.

Why are we humans so easily convinced there might be a better way than God's way? Why am I so easily persuaded that if God really loves me, He would want me to have what I really want? How is it possible that we dare question whether God is keeping back the best stuff for Himself alone? Eve was induced to believe those things. Do we . . . even just a little? Why do appearances (she saw that the fruit was lovely to look at) matter so much to us? Why does pleasure, that part of life we'd like to "taste" for ourselves (she surmised that it would taste good), hold such allure? Why does being in the know (she obviously had an inquiring mind) make us feel so proud of ourselves? Why do we listen to the wrong voices? Why do we choose the way that *seems right* or maybe even settle for one that seems just *all right,* when God has told us what the right choice is and has warned us where other choices will lead? God wasn't exaggerating when He said, "There is a way that seems right to a man, but in the end it leads to death." Why do those who were made in the very image of the Creator—made *by God, out of God, for God*—act so very ungodlike? And why, oh why, does He love us in spite of it?

THE PRICE IS RIGHT

It didn't take long for Adam and Eve to realize their mistake when they ate what was offered by Satan. Immediately upon eating the forbidden fruit, God's humans felt shame at the state in which they found themselves: now *nakedly* out of sync with their holy God. Closely following shame, Adam and Eve recognized their inability to face holiness in such a condition. Should they try to hide what they had done? How about camouflaging it? Quick, make like a fig tree! Maybe God wouldn't recognize them or even see them if they were well hidden or at least cleverly disguised. It was a good try. Yet, in spite of their best efforts at concealment, the Lord located the covert duo. There was only one thing left for them to try: denial. Most of us like to think we are fairly adept at keeping ourselves covered, but we're not any more original than Adam and Eve when we try to evade God's discovery of our sins. Nor are we any more creative than they when we refuse to take responsibility for our actions. If caught, blame someone else, anyone else.

When God came looking for His children (and do revel in the knowledge that He came looking for them, even in their sinful state, and do take note, because this certainly won't be the only time!), He found not only shame and concealment; He found Adam and Eve's outright refusal to admit to their part in the collapse of their world. Eve blamed the serpent, and Adam blamed Eve. Well, Adam actually kind of blamed God for giving him Eve, who gave him the fruit. Just how far can one fall?

At this point it was left to God to tell all the participants in this sinful encounter what the results would be for them and for those who would come after them. And the results were devastating.

Because of the serpent's participation in the debacle, God cursed him to bite the dust for the rest of his life.

And because of mankind's sin, God cursed the ground, His beautiful creation, His perfect garden.

What sorrow God must have felt when ultimately He turned His attention to the main characters in the drama. Eve would suffer a righteous punishment for the mother of the earth. Her "job" given in the beginning was to fill the world with off-spring. That same offspring would now be the vessel through which Eve would be punished. Much pain would accompany delivering and raising the sons of men. Adam's punishment was righteous as well. With a cursed ground, with painful, sweat-producing toil, with thorns and thistles outmaneuvering the crops he would plant, Adam's job, assigned to him in the beginning by God as a blessing, would now be a burden. And on top of their individual punishments, God's two loved ones would be banished from the wondrous garden into another landscape, a harsh and forbidding one. Adam and Eve had been offered the good life, "where the living is easy," inside God's world. These humans had been *divinely fashioned* to live in a world laid out just for them. They were not designed to survive life on the outside. Inside God's world, inside God's will, inside God's way—that's the good life, the life intended for mankind. Life outside God's world, outside God's will, outside God's way is always going to be arduous. In that hard place, God's children would begin to die a long, lingering, laborious death.

> *Life outside God's world, outside God's will, outside God's way is always going to be arduous.*

That's a really high price to pay for sin. But it was a really big sin. Adam and Eve had been confronted with a choice: believe God or believe anything else. They chose to believe the "else." He had told them an "or else" would follow if they disobeyed His command about the tree, but they listened to something else instead of listening to God. We need to understand that sin is choosing *anything else* but God. There is no *other* way.

"The End" Begins

What would be our fate if God had stopped our story there? Unimaginable! Thank God, and I mean that quite literally, this is only the beginning of God's narrative. It's merely the background for the greatest story ever told. Because God didn't deal just with the sin of His children during that fateful encounter in the garden: He dealt with sin itself.

> *God didn't deal just with the sin of His children during that fateful encounter in the garden: He dealt with sin itself.*

The Almighty turned to His enemy, the initiator of sin, and He pronounced upon Satan a fate worse than death. He pronounced upon him *failure.* God told Satan, the grasping one who wanted to rule both heaven and earth in God's place, that he would not win this war he had started against the Holy One and His children. God told Satan he would go down in humiliating defeat. And the instrument of his destruction would be One who would come from the very woman whom Satan took as his first prisoner of war. God acknowledged that it would be a terrible conflict. There would be devastating injuries inflicted on both sides in the combat, but in the end, in spite of punishing, bruising wounds, the Seed of the woman would stand victorious over the fallen body and the crushed head of the serpent.

And so the battle began.

4 THE FIRST OF THE WORST

THE WAGES OF SIN

There is a way that seems right to a man,
but in the end it leads to death.

—PROVERBS 14:12

GENESIS 4–11

I am what you might call a creative cook. I consider a recipe a mere suggestion rather than a dogma. Measurements can be approximately correct, flavors can be enhanced with more (or maybe just more exotic) seasoning, and if certain ingredients are unavailable, improvising is acceptable. I've had some resounding successes where eaters gave rave reviews. And I've had some unmitigated disasters that have resulted in my slinking out of a church potluck with an embarrassingly uneaten casserole.

Almost any decision can seem like a good idea at the time.

It must have seemed right, or at least all right, that fateful day when God's first children made their first executive decision. After all, the argument had been persuasive, and the persuader had been eloquent, and God had previously seemed so agreeable about things. Who was to know that it could all go so wrong so fast?

In a blur of pronouncements, judgment had fallen hard and swift upon those who had disobeyed. Sentenced to a hard life and a certain death, Adam and Eve found themselves on the way out. (The God who *is* justice *must* punish sin.) What would happen to the humans in that cruel, unforgiving world that had been described for

43

them by their loving God? Thorns would pierce their delicate skin, hard labor would bend their backs, and the burdens of surviving in a world not made for them would eventually destroy the bodies God had so tenderly molded. If the God who loved and protected from sin was also the God who couldn't be in the presence of sin and the God who judged those who sinned, who would save the people from their fate?

God would.

Marvel at that. The God who judges is the same God who saves from judgment! For protection from the world they would enter and as a promise that things would eventually be made right (that's also justice!), God removed Adam's and Eve's temporary, fig-leaf clothing, which could in no way shield them from the consequences of their sin, and He covered His tender children in animal skins. That first shedding of innocent blood was to cover the effects, the consequences, the destructive power of sin. What a statement of who God is! Holy God who can have no part in sin and will surely judge those who traffic in sin is the same God who loves his children enough to save them from sin, even if that means someone else has to pay the price in their place! Atonement: the covering of sin by the shedding of blood. Clues, hints, and foreshadowings that indicate how far God will go one day to save his children. Don't you love it! From the very beginning, a plan of salvation was in place. God knew when they bit into sin that the children would need someone to save them. And He would be that Savior.

The God who judges is the same God who saves from judgment!

As a final act concurrent with banishing Adam and Eve to the world outside the garden, God effectively shut down access to the other tree that stood alongside the tree of knowledge in the center of His world. The tree of life, the fruit of which would have allowed mankind to live forever in perfection, must not be available to man in his current condition of sinfulness. What a horror it would be if man lived forever while sin ate away at him. So, in an act of love, God placed guardian cherubim with a flashing sword to bar the way to the tree of life, the tree that was *offered* but not *chosen.* And covered in mercy by skins probably still oozing the lifeblood of one who was sacrificed for their sin, Adam and Eve were cast out of God's garden and ushered into a world where they would begin to die.

BROTHERLY HATE

When Adam and Eve left the garden, they walked into a war zone. Satan had declared war on God's creation, and God had declared war on Satan because of it. That war was, is, and will be cataclysmic, and nothing less than the fate of the universe hangs in the balance. Adam and Eve entered a world controlled by a denounced, doomed, and desperate enemy. God had assured Satan that he would not win the war and, in fact, would be mortally wounded and eventually crushed. But the Evil One would not go down without a fight. He would do anything to try to outlast his death sentence.

As Genesis 4 opens, Adam and Eve have produced their firstborn son and named him Cain. The birth of a baby is filled with expectation and hope. Eve even acknowledged that he came with the help of the Lord. Did she believe or at least fervently wish that this apparent gift from God might alleviate some of the pain of her miserable condition? If that was her hope, she was to be sadly disheartened. Raising Cain never leads to good results. Eve's next son, Abel, soon followed, and both boys took their places in the fallen world where their parents lived and toiled. The young men took up jobs: Abel as a shepherd and Cain as a farmer in a land that, because of the curse upon it, made farming difficult. Maybe that explains what happened next.

We don't know when man began to make offerings to God or what the circumstances were, but in the course of time Cain and Abel both brought offerings to the Lord. God must have asked men to do it and indicated how they should do it, because it appears that everyone in the story of Cain and Abel and God knew what was expected. I've heard different explanations for why God accepted Abel's offering and rejected Cain's, but the truth is we're not fully told. God doesn't have to tell us why He does things, and frequently He doesn't. Many who are far more learned than I am in the Scriptures and original languages believe it was supposed to be a sin offering, for which God demanded the shedding of blood. If that was the case, then Cain obviously didn't come seeking atonement, and God would certainly have rejected his lack of contrition.

I'm convinced there's also a clear message here even for those of us who are not versed in the original languages or on sacrificial rituals. Later in Scripture, instructions for acceptable grain offerings are outlined, so either Cain's timing was wrong or something else was wrong. Verses 3–4 of Genesis 4 might give us a clue to what was wrong in Cain's offering: "In the course of time Cain brought forth *some* of the fruits of the soil as an offering to the LORD. But Abel brought *fat portions* from some of the *firstborn* of his flock." I ask my fifth graders a question when we read that Scripture: what is the difference between "some" and "fat portions from . . . the firstborn"? The kids recognize immediately that there was a difference in the degree of the offering. I think there was also a difference in the *heart* of the offering. There are times when God doesn't seem nearly as impressed with *what* we do as *why* we do it. How often do I plop "something" on the altar because I know I'm supposed to and then hope that God doesn't notice I have withheld the "fat" and "firstborn"? What does it tell God about my heart toward Him when I can't be bothered, can't be trusted to give back to Him my very best offering?

What Cain offered, or didn't offer, and why Cain offered told God where his heart was in relation to God Himself. Maybe Cain resented the Lord wanting offerings in the first place. After all, God had withheld from him the benefits of living in that perfect garden. Maybe Cain didn't see himself as particularly sinful or didn't care if he was, so why bother making an offering for sin? God had already punished them all pretty heavily for sin anyway. Because farming was hard work and crops were possibly scarce, maybe Cain decided to keep the best for himself as his just reward. After all, who wants leftovers when you're the one who did the work? There's also the chance that the older brother resented his goody-two-shoes younger brother, who always did everything right, and Cain decided to show everyone he couldn't be bossed and bullied into acquiescing like Abel did. (You may have noticed that each of these possible excuses is not much different than those we still offer today.) All we really know is that something was wrong in Cain's offering. Wrong offering or wrong heart, it was just *wrong,* and God had the *right* to reject it.

Whatever Cain's reason for refusing to do it God's way, God's rejection of his offering rankled Cain, and he became angry and sullenly resentful. When God confronted him about his postoffering funk, He warned Cain that sin was just waiting to get him in its grip. And we do know this about Cain: sin certainly did grip him!

Adam's elder son invited his younger brother to go into the field with him, and there Cain killed Abel. It was pre-meditated, cold-blooded murder. How rapidly sin can escalate, building on itself. Sullen anger, feelings of rejection, resentment for the way we are treated, blame for how things have gone, and boom! Someone else is forced to pay the price for our problem. Cain made Abel pay the ultimate cost for his own pain and anger.

Notice what happened next. Just as God went looking for Adam and Eve after their sin, He went looking for Cain after his, and just as before, God went with a question for the sinner.

When God pursued Adam and Eve to the place they were hiding, He asked them, "Where are you?" God was where He always was, in a place they could find Him if they wanted. But their relationship with God was seriously out of whack, and they were separated from Him by their sinfulness. Maybe God's question to Adam and Eve meant "Where are you in relation to me?"

When God went after Cain, His question was "Where is your brother?" Maybe God's question to Cain meant "Where are you in relation to your brother?"

It becomes increasingly obvious as Scripture progresses—when the Law is given in the Old Testament and when Jesus sums up the Law in the New Testament—that God values the relationship we have with Him and the relationship we have with our brothers and sisters above all things. When He goes seeking a sinner, God needs the sinner to know which of those valued relationships has been damaged or severed.

As a result of Cain's sin and his callous refusal to admit any responsibility for his brother's well-being, God sent Cain packing from the land that had received his brother's blood. He also placed a curse on Cain. God, in His justice, has to deal harshly with sin. It's His nature to do so. Cain was driven away, out of God's presence, to face Satan's world alone. No wonder Cain begged until the just God, who is also the merciful and loving God, agreed to place a mark on him, warning anyone Cain encountered not to deal with him as he had dealt with his own brother. Then to thank God for His mercy, Cain went off into Satan's world and produced a race of people who would do Satan himself proud. What a guy!

"I've Fallen, and I Can't Get Up"

And what a world God's little children found themselves inhabiting, a world that belonged heart and soul to the Evil One, the sworn enemy of the Holy God. Perhaps one reason the world became so evil was that God had told Satan he would be defeated by the Seed of the woman. Not being all-knowing like God, how could Satan know which seed *the* Seed would come from? He had taken care of Abel through the actions of his servant Cain, and the Seed couldn't come through Cain, who was banished from the presence of God and had quite enthusiastically gone over to the dark side. So how was Satan going to find his potential destroyer? One solution for his dilemma, and it was a pretty effective one, was to infect the entire race with sin.

So a bad world got worse. And worse. And worse. The first part of Genesis 6 is deeply disquieting. First we read "the sons of God saw that the daughters of men were beautiful." Here we go again—it's the shiny tree thing! "And they married any of them they chose." God's children mixed themselves up with sworn enemies and really bad kinfolk and, some scholars believe, even demons in unholy matrimony.

The Almighty purposely began to limit the life span of mankind, but people were still able to do prolific damage even with a shorter time in which to do it. It got really, really wretched as time went on. We can't begin to imagine how detestable it must have become to lead to what's described in Genesis 6:5: "The LORD saw how great man's wickedness on the earth had become, and that every inclination of the thoughts of his heart was only evil all the time." Read that: *every . . . thought* (of the brain), *every . . . inclination* (instinct, leaning) of the *heart* (that which governs thought and action) was *only evil . . . all* the time. Could it get any worse than that?

We know that Holy God is going to act in this situation. It would be out of the question for Him, because of who He is, not to do something about it. But before He would act against evil, the Lord God would hold to the pattern He'd established in the garden generations before. He would first warn.

There are two things worth noting in Genesis 5 before God acts in Genesis 6. Years ago one of the most incredible preachers I've ever heard preached one of the most interesting sermons I've ever listened to, based on one of the most boring chapters in the Bible I'd never really read. He preached an entire sermon on Genesis 5, which is nothing but a genealogical account of the descendants from Adam to Noah. Turns out it is really a bit more than that.

Genealogies in the Bible are important for at least a couple of reasons. They trace the Seed of the woman through generations to validate His ancestry. For another, a list of names in the Bible always reminds me that individuals matter very much to God. In Paul's letters he listed individuals who were important to him for reasons he never

> *A list of names in the Bible always reminds me that individuals matter very much to God.*

told us, and the book of Nehemiah reels off names of individuals who mattered enough to Nehemiah that they had to be mentioned.

So Genesis 5 would be significant for those reasons alone, but in this particular genealogy, I point out two names to my kids every year—Enoch and his son Methuselah—and they make this much more than just a genealogy. Anyone reading the chapter would notice what was different about Enoch. The account of every other man listed in the chapter ends the same: "and then he died." But of Enoch it is said he "walked with God; then he was no more, because God took him away." He's even mentioned in Hebrews 11 in the roster of the faithful for the very same reason. He was set apart from every other individual of his time because, in a wretchedly wicked world sliding toward oblivion, Enoch stood out as a beacon, a faithful man in the midst of rampant unfaithfulness. It was as if God couldn't bear to leave the only good man in that hideous world. Or maybe it was for another reason. Maybe He hoped people would notice Enoch's disappearance and notice the God who had snatched him away.

But before God took him, Enoch did one other thing that we know of. He fathered a son whom he named Methuselah. If people have heard anything about Methuselah, they know he is the oldest man listed in the Bible. He has, in fact, become synonymous with getting old, as in "he is as old as Methuselah." But if you read Genesis 5, you might notice one other thing about Methuselah. He was the grandfather of Noah, who would play a prominent part in God's coming judgment. What I never knew before the sermon, and what makes Methuselah really interesting, is that the godly Enoch gave his first son a name that God could use to teach a lesson. *Methuselah* seems to be a combination of words meaning "death" and "God will judge." Put it together and you get a warning: when Methuselah dies, God will judge. I also understand, though my math skills rank right up there with my knowledge of Hebrew, that if you add up the numbers, you will find that Methuselah died the same year the flood came. The man who lived longer than any other man we know of was a living early-warning device to everyone else. For 969 years Methuselah served as a portent of what would happen if people didn't change their ways.

But just as they didn't notice when God took Enoch off the face of the earth, the inhabitants of a wicked world didn't notice what Enoch's son was telling them. God was going to take righteous action if mankind didn't take the right actions.

With the earth hurtling toward oblivion at warp speed, Genesis 6 tells the story of a creation gone totally wrong. God looked down on the deplorable condition of the world He had created, at the depths to which His children had sunk, and He was "grieved," and "his heart was filled with pain." And the Lord decided to "wipe mankind, whom I have created, from the face of the earth." Uh-oh.

BARN VOYAGE

One of my favorite things in the Scriptures is how often matters hinge on one well-placed word. In the middle of God's decision to wipe the whole of mankind from the face of the earth, something changed His mind. "But Noah."

The flood is the story of judgment; the ark is the story of grace.

Have you ever wondered what would have happened if there hadn't been a "but"? It was all over, "*but Noah* found favor in the eyes of the LORD." In the midst of the evil that God saw, He also saw Noah: righteous, blameless, and, like his great-grandfather Enoch, walking with God when no one else did. This is one of the times when we see why God gave man the ability to choose. In the midst of all the bad was the beautiful. How it must have filled the heart of God with joy to see that Noah had chosen the right way. And may we all rejoice because of Noah as well. The total annihilation of mankind was averted by one who chose God.

The chronicle of Noah and the ark, like all the other stories in the Bible, is the story of God. It is the record of how God will go to any extent to save His people. The flood is the story of judgment; the ark is the story of grace. Noah, by faith, believed God's promise to save him and built a boat to God's specifications with plans to carry the cargo God chose. The building of a boat in a dry land was a warning to the people of the world much like the name Methuselah was. For more than a hundred years, Noah built and preached about what was coming. For nearly a thousand years, Methuselah's name reminded of the surety of God's judgment. God kept Noah building, and He kept Methuselah living, giving people opportunity to hear the message of righteousness and make the righteous choice. But when time was up, only eight people and a floating barn full of animals would escape God's wrath.

And what wrath God unleashed upon the creation that had rejected Him. He used the world He had made to destroy itself. The springs of the great deep burst forth! And the floodgates of heaven were opened! Water poured from the sky, and water gushed from the ground. The rains came down, and the floods came up. And God judged the creation He had made. Because God is perfect, He has the right to judge, and because God creates, He has the right to destroy His creation. The Just Judge ruled, and the Creator destroyed.

And then, to further demonstrate who He is, God saved mankind with the same water He used to destroy mankind. The very floods that washed away and drowned those who had refused to choose God also floated and carried to safety those God chose to save. Humankind was saved by the venue of water through faith in God's promise that He would save. And the saving water finally deposited God's passengers on the mountains of Ararat, and after a year of floating, Noah and his family finally set foot again on solid ground.

If you had been inside a bobbing box for a year and seventeen days with all your relatives and every animal in the world, plus all the by-products of same, what would you have done first? The first response is a heart response. When my husband returns home from frequent trips to Europe, Canada, or even New York, the first thing he does is go for Mexican food. It is dear to his heart, and he has missed it. If your first response is a heart response, what is the first thing you would have done after climbing off the ark? The first thing Noah did was build an altar and make an offering to the God who had saved him. Good choice!

After Noah got off the ark, God gave him his marching orders to fill the earth again with people. He also ushered him into a different kind of world. In Genesis 9, God intimated to Noah that the relationship between man and animals would not be the same as it had been. Whereas Adam had named the animals, seemingly communed with them, and lived in vegetarian peace with them, the new world would be more of a dog-eat-dog world, and man would become a carnivore as well.

I remember an old episode of *Cheers* when the character Norm was asked how he was doing, and he replied, "It's a dog-eat-dog world, and I feel like I'm wearing Milk-Bone underwear!" I wonder if Noah had a similar feeling when he faced the aftermath of the flood. At least he had been warned that if he went after the "dogs," whether or not to eat them, they just might bite back!

It also appears that after filling the land with people again, some sort of human government would be set up and would have the authority to shed the blood of any person who shed the blood of another. It seems, by this particular admonition, that wiping sinners off the face of the earth hadn't eliminated sin. Probably because eight sinners walked off the ark.

Knowing that every inclination of man's heart is evil from childhood, God obviously knew a time would come when He would have to deal with the effects of sin again. But He promised that He would never again destroy all living creatures as He had just done, that seasons would continue to change and day would continue to follow night, and that He would deal with the problem of evil in a different way.

The Lord established that covenant with humankind and told Noah the sign of the covenant would be His rainbow, a pretty great symbol. A rainbow is caused by the refraction of light through water and dust particles in the air. God's light bounces off all the debris, scatters in all directions, and turns mere dust and vapor into something beautiful. I like this part too: God said, "Whenever I bring clouds over the earth and the rainbow appears in the clouds [like a beacon of bright promise in hazy times], I will remember my covenant. . . . I will see it and remember."

> *When God looks at the rainbow, He remembers the promise He made to man.*

When *God* looks at the rainbow, *He* remembers the promise He made to man, His covenant with the earth's inhabitants. When *I* look at the rainbow, what do I remember? I remember that God always remembers, and I remember that God always keeps His promises! He is, and He is remembering.

After receiving God's promise, Noah and his family embarked upon the adventure of living in a brand-new world. Looking out across the face of the devastated earth, they must have been able to see where sin had led. One would think, unless one was familiar with human nature, that the flood would have been sufficient to get mankind immediately and permanently upon the right track. Surely people had learned that God's way was best. Surely they respected His desires that they scatter across the new world and fill the land with people. Surely they had decided that their worship should be only of the God who had delivered them. You think?

BABBLE ON

Genesis 11 opens with people moving. At least they got the first part right. The problem seems to be that they were all moving in the same direction. Was that going to fill the whole world? And then they stopped moving when they found a particular plain they liked, a plain in what would become Babylon. Instead of moving on, the people settled there. They said to one another, "Come, let us build ourselves a city, with a tower that reaches to the heavens, so that we may make a name for ourselves and not be scattered." Humans decided to ignore God's desires, invent their own religion to reach God by their own efforts on their own terms, and make themselves look pretty great in the process. They even decided to make their own bricks instead of using the much stronger stones God had made. Isn't self-sufficiency a wonderful thing!

In spite of the willfulness of men, the will of God will be done.

However, God wasted no time in dealing with this rebellion. He "came down" to see the tower that men were building to reach Him. And then He not only changed their building plans; He changed their plans to stay together and ignore His plans for them. He "confused" their languages so they confused each other, and then He scattered them over the face of the whole earth. So there! In spite of the willfulness of men, the will of God will be done.

After the creation of a perfect world in Genesis 2, the nine chapters that follow, a chronicle of sin for sure, demonstrate that with the notable exceptions of Enoch and Noah, mankind had proven itself notoriously inept at the choice thing. What was a good God to do when humans kept making the wrong choices?

God would make a choice of His own.

5 PROMISES, PROMISES

THE CALL OF ABRAHAM

For I have chosen him that he will direct his children
and his household after him
to keep the way of the Lord by doing what is right and just.

—GENESIS 18:19

GENESIS 12–22

One of the funniest things I've ever witnessed was a vigorous performance of the song, "Father Abraham," sung by my parents, their grandchildren, and my sister's in-laws. The most hilarious part is when the actions call for head bobbing, arms seesawing wildly, feet moving in a maniacal march, and all the time the body spinning like a whirling dervish. If you have ever engaged in this ritual, you can verify both the cardio benefits you receive and the dizzying effect it has on your equilibrium. In the case of the gyrating grandparents, we nearly had to call the paramedics to resuscitate both progenitors and progeny. They were nearly dead, and we all nearly died laughing!

I assume, however, that it is more entertaining to sing about father Abraham than it would have been to be father Abraham.

A friend recently suggested that my language concerning Abraham was a bit "lofty" (what a great word!). She may have been hinting that I am more cavalier about some of God's other servants, or she may have (rightly) assumed that I am a bit in awe of Abraham. There are some characters in the Bible who make us feel okay about who we are and where we stand. I like those guys. But there are other individuals whom we watch in wonder as they exhibit a kind of faithfulness we can only imagine. Abraham is one of those.

A Plan to Man

The first eleven chapters of Genesis provide quite a variety in scenery. The first chapter contains the magnificent account of creation, where the word *God* is mentioned thirty times. The second chapter recounts the tender story of God's special care with the garden and the people He put in it, and the name *Lord God* is mentioned eleven times. These opening chapters portray a beautiful world where our loving God was in charge and mankind was in love with Him.

But with the advent of sin in Genesis 3, the focus shifts temporarily from the Creator to the creature, and the scene gets ugly fast. The chapters that follow paint a gloomy picture of where mankind rapidly and willingly went when they ignored God. I know God is merciful, and, believe me, I revel in His mercy for me and mine, but I have a hard time understanding His forbearance for a world so unrepentantly wicked as that one (and maybe even this one). Yet finally, after the pain of reading Genesis 3–11 and seeing where humanity's choices had led, with great pleasure I turn the page in my Bible and see the Almighty (like a divine version of James Brown) say, "Watch Me work now!"

God's plan wasn't a new plan. It wasn't something He came up with because what He had been doing wasn't working.

In Genesis 12, God once again gets intimately involved in the affairs of mankind. He had promised back in the garden that He would take care of sin and the instigator of sin. From the seed of the woman would come the one who would crush the head of the serpent and destroy his power over creation. God's plan wasn't a new plan. It wasn't something He came up with because what He had been doing wasn't working. It's just that in Genesis 12, He decided to let a few humans in on His strategy.

The Almighty's ultimate plan involved making a nation that would be His chosen people, chosen not because they were special but because their purpose as a nation was.

Theirs would be a momentous and essential purpose, a holy purpose. This nation would be God's instrument both to bring the Seed into the world and to demonstrate God's nature to the world. I remind my kids over and over of the dual purpose of God's people, because our purpose as God's people today is the same.

Two thousand years have passed, and powerful nations have inhabited earth. For hundreds of years there had been impressive accomplishments by amazingly advanced civilizations: Stonehenge in England, bronze ornaments and tools in China, geometry and astronomy in Babylon, and even the tremendous engineering feats that are the pyramids of Egypt. It's interesting that the Bible never touches on other world powers except where they affect His nation. Just remember, God is telling *His story.* Our great God didn't designate one of the already-established nations to be His chosen people. He didn't choose a nation already powerful within itself. Instead, God chose the right man and began to build the right nation—a nation He would use to accomplish His plan for all nations.

Go West, Not-So-Young Man

In a Bible full of heroes used by God to accomplish great things for Him, some individuals stand out from the rest. Even these standouts weren't perfect by any means, but their lives were foundational in carrying out God's plan. Our tendency is to think that God would call only those people who are already serving Him or are at least prone to serving Him—people like Noah, who was righteous, blameless, and walking with God. Yet the Lord called Moses out of exile in the Midianite desert, Gideon out of hiding in a cave, Paul out of tormenting Christians, and He called Abraham out of idolatry. Why wouldn't God summon someone who was already "doing it right"? Maybe there wasn't anyone. Or maybe God did what He did so we would look at people like Abraham and see not the man's goodness but God's! Why He called Abraham only He knows, but we're privileged to marvel at what God called Abraham to believe and do.

Abraham (called Abram at the time) was a wealthy man in a flourishing civilization when God called him. God required Abraham to do two things immediately. First, He told Abraham to "leave." He was to leave that flourishing civilization, his wealthy family, the people he knew, all the things he depended on. He was to leave behind what had shaped him and made him successful by his culture's standards.

Second, God told Abraham to "go." He didn't tell Abraham where he was going; He just told him to go. And proving to us that God had indeed made a good choice, Abraham did two things: he left, and he went.

In Hebrews 11:8 we read, "By faith Abraham, when called to go . . . obeyed and went, even though he did not know where he was going." It's important to reiterate to my fifth graders that Abraham didn't know where he was going, but he chose to follow who was leading him. This is what I want them to learn above all else. The *Who* is worth following *wherever* He leads. All Abraham had was his faith in who God is. That's why I want my kids to know those characteristics of God's nature that

> *The Who is worth following wherever He leads.*

we learn the first week of class. I beat my hands on those symbols representing God's character so many times during the year that the cards are usually stained and need replacing by the next year. I want it to become a conviction for the students. I want them to know God so they will want to follow Him as Abraham did.

Abraham believed God and believed that God knew what He was doing and where He was leading, and Abraham put himself in God's hands. That is faith. That's what we need as well if we are to leave what binds us to our world and go forward into the world that God promises will give us great blessing.

From the very beginning of the story of Abraham, we see the trait with which he would become synonymous. Abraham's faith was even more extraordinary when we consider he didn't actually know God in the beginning. But Abraham *chose* to *believe in* God, and he chose to *believe* God. It's the same thing God requires from us: believe He *is,* believe He *can,* and believe He *will.*

And God invited Abraham to believe some incredible things. He told Abraham from the very beginning of their relationship that He had big plans for him: through Abraham would come a great land, a great name, a great nation, and a great blessing for all nations of the earth. God "announced the gospel in advance to Abraham: 'All nations will be blessed through you.'" It's remarkable that Abraham's faith continued undiminished when he saw not one of those promises completely fulfilled. Lofty language or not, that's pretty awesome.

God's covenant with Abraham, the equivalent of swearing an oath, was in Abraham's day usually initiated by a person of high standing with one who was subject to him. That covenant would bind Abraham to God throughout his life. Abraham chose to believe that God would fulfill every detail of His covenant, and he acted upon his belief in his God. That must have been why he was chosen.

Abraham was seventy-five years old when God called him, but he packed up his life—thousands of animals, hundreds of pounds of possessions, a plethora of servants, one nephew, and one wife—and he started out for, as it turned out, the Promised Land. From place to place Abraham went at God's direction, and in each place he stopped, he built an altar to the God who led him onward. And as Abraham traveled on in faith, God began showing His faithfulness to His covenant. The Lord blessed Abraham, and He blessed those who blessed him, and He cursed those who cursed him, and He made Abraham rich and famous.

A "Lot" of Bad Moves

In the middle of Abraham's travels with God, we have the story of his nephew Lot and what happens when a pilgrim quits moving and settles down. It's a cautionary tale for those of us who sometimes weary of the journey God would lead us on. When Abraham became so blessed that it caused a problem with his nephew, who also was blessed just for going with Abraham, the two men separated and went their own ways. Well, one of them *went*. The other kind of *stayed.* The story illustrates what happens when we quit moving with God and decide to make our home in the comfortable world we're supposed to be passing through.

In Genesis 13, Lot took his possessions, set out *toward* the east, lived *among* the cities of the plains, and pitched his tents *near* Sodom. He first cast his vision in the direction of the iniquitous metropolis, then hung out among the inhabitants, and soon settled in the suburbs. I don't imagine that at the time Lot had any intention of moving into that wicked city. Maybe he just wanted to be near the grocery store and the mall. Then, oops! Lot was soon living *in* Sodom. Okay, it was probably more convenient than running into town every time he needed to pick up something. It doesn't mean he condoned what was going on in the

The story illustrates what happens when we quit moving with God and decide to make our home in the comfortable world we're supposed to be passing through.

big, bad city just because he was *living* there! Well, then, how would he explain that the next time we see him, he was sitting in the gateway of the city, where officials met with other important participants to discuss city business? But you know what? I bet Lot could have given an answer that sounded good. That's the way we humans are. We can convince ourselves that whatever we want is good for us.

It's possible that Lot didn't realize how involved he had gotten. That's also typical of us. If a person had asked him years before if he was at least having a good influence on the people around him, Lot might have grasped at that straw as a reason for his being there. He probably would have considered it an egregious exaggeration if someone had told him that the day would soon come when, even though he was convinced of imminent judgment on Sodom, an angel would have to take him by the hand and drag him out of the city right before God rained down fire. Moreover, Lot never would have believed that when he fled God's judgment, he would take no one out with him except the three women he took in, and they narrowly escaped. And would Lot have ever conceived that one he took in with him, his wife, would have become so attached to Sodom that she would risk it all (and lose it all) to look longingly back, yearning for the "other" way, regretting to leave the "exciting" life behind? And who would have given any credence to the notion that Lot, drunk and oblivious, would father his own grandchildren after it was all over? There are some places the mind just won't go. I don't imagine anything of the sort entered Lot's mind as he took his possessions all those many years ago and, tired of traveling even with God leading, decided to make a place for himself in the "outside" world.

GREAT EXPECTATIONS

Meanwhile, Abraham journeyed where God led and stopped when God directed and built altars for offerings, which God honored. And he waited. And he waited some more. Abraham waited for God to fulfill His promise, to honor His covenant. The patriarch gets perfect marks from me for his patience. I have trouble waiting twenty-four minutes for my dentist appointment. Twenty-four hours is endless when I'm waiting for a repairman. Twenty-four days for a back order? Who needs it? But Abraham waited on God for twenty-four years! During twenty-four years of waiting, the Lord frequently reminded Abraham that he would be the father of many descendants and that through his descendants would come a blessing for all descendants of all mankind. God even suggested Abraham try to count the stars if he wanted to see just how many offspring would call him father.

There was only one problem with God's promise: Abraham had no offspring to produce any descendants. Okay, his patience slipped every now and then. (Yeah! He was human!) The aging man named his servant Eliezer his heir until God told him that his heir would be a son from his own body. So Abraham acquiesced when his wife, Sarah, sent her servant Hagar to him, thus producing Ishmael, an heir from his own body who would become a lifelong thorn in the side of his real heirs. But finally Abraham's waiting paid off. Twenty-four years after God called Abraham into a covenant relationship and promised that he would become the father of a nation, God called on Abraham to tell him the time had come for the covenant to be confirmed and for Abraham to become that father.

When God visited Abraham after many years of waiting, He confirmed that nations and kings would come from Abraham. He confirmed that the land of Canaan, where Abraham was now an alien traveler, would belong to his descendants. He confirmed that He would remain Abraham's God and the God of his children after him. He confirmed that He expected Abraham and his offspring to keep the covenant as well and that the sign of their keeping covenant would be the act of circumcision, a physical sign of spiritually belonging to God forever since there was no undoing it. God called it "My covenant in your flesh . . . an everlasting covenant." The Lord confirmed that all this would happen, that indeed an heir would come from Abraham's body, and that the heir would eventually produce a huge body of believers.

And furthermore, God confirmed that the heir would also come from the body of Abraham's beloved Sarah. *That's* when Abraham laughed. He probably couldn't help it. The old man undoubtedly pictured his little ninety-year-old wife, and he couldn't do anything but laugh at the inconceivability of it all. Was it possible for a hundred-year-old man and a ninety-year-old woman to conceive and bear a child? No, it wasn't. It was impossible. *Can it happen?* No. *But will it happen?* Just believe it, Abraham.

So Abraham, being Abraham, the man who always believed God, did what God told him to do. First, he had himself and every man in his household circumcised as a confirmation of his agreement to keep covenant with God. And then when the time came and God told him to go, one more time Abraham went where he was directed: into Sarah's tent.

I'm not a voyeur, but I would like to have heard the conversation that followed Abraham pulling back the flap and entering Sarah's bedchamber. Do you reckon the giggles that began with God's announcement continued in the tent? I'm guessing that *amazement* doesn't begin to describe their wonder at the Good Lord's awesome power!

No Laughing Matter

Abraham and Sarah obeyed God and trusted His ability to keep a promise that seemed unachievable. Their faith resulted in a son they named Isaac. What Abraham and Sarah did was impossible, and they *knew* it. That is, it was impossible unless a person knew a God who reveled in proving that nothing is impossible with Him. And Abraham was a man who *knew God.*

> *If Abraham was ever tempted to question God's faithfulness in keeping promises, all he had to do was look at the face of his beloved son.*

Don't you imagine that Isaac was the delight of his parents? He was a miracle, pure and simple—a walking, talking reminder of what God can and will do, the first real "proof" that God truly intended to honor His covenant agreement. Even the meaning of Isaac's name, "he laughs," reflected the joy and incredulity of his arrival. Isaac was the son of promise, the long-awaited child on which everything else would depend. If Abraham ever wavered in his faith or in his belief in God's goodness to him, if he was ever tempted to question God's faithfulness in keeping promises, all he had to do was look at the face of his beloved son, and he would remember. Abraham would know that God was all he believed Him to be.

Try then to imagine what Abraham must have thought and felt when God called on him one day and asked him to do the really unbelievable. When God had asked him to leave everything he knew and counted on, when God had asked him to go into the unknown, when God had led him *through* but never really *to* the Promised Land, when God had invited him to believe the impossible was possible, had Abraham not proved his faith in God and his own faithfulness to the covenant? Had this oft-tested man of faith not passed every test God had given him? He had. But God had one more test for Abraham, and it was a big one.

The very nature of the relationship between God and Abraham would be tested. God would find out, and so would Abraham, just how much Abraham believed, just how far he would extend his faith in who God is.

An "Altared" Man

The Father of all spoke to this father of one and told him, "Take your son, your only son, Isaac, whom you love, and go to the region of Moriah. Sacrifice him there as a burnt offering on one of the mountains I will tell you about." Now *that's* a test. Abraham was asked some soul-wrenching questions in God's testing. Will you believe? Will you submit? Will you cast everything on God, Abraham? Will you trust everything to God, Abraham? Will you offer up to God everything on which you have based your trust?

Once again Abraham was asked to go to a place only God would know, and this time he was asked to do a thing only God could understand. Abraham was asked to make the ultimate offering to God. Upon the altar of God, he was asked to place every hope he had. God had told him that Isaac was the son of promise, the one through whom everything would come: the promised nation and the promised blessing to all nations and lands. Would Abraham be willing to give up that visible symbol of blessing, that in-the-flesh proof that his God was a covenant-keeping, trustworthy, truly-worth-following God?

In answer, Abraham, now altered by decades of faith in God, went where He directed, built an altar, bound and placed his son—his only son whom he loved— upon the altar, and raised the knife to slay him.

The imposing faith Abraham demonstrated during this, his greatest test, is revealed in language that seems almost sparse in its scriptural rendering. When Abraham and Isaac went to make the offering, Abraham told the servants who accompanied them, "Stay here while I and the boy go over there. We will worship and then *we will come back to you.*" How did he "know"? Then, again, when Isaac asked where the lamb for the burnt offering was, Abraham replied, "God himself *will provide* the lamb." That's quite an assumption if he didn't "know" something. (Also, I wonder if Abraham had the slightest idea that he was foretelling the future when God would indeed provide the Lamb.)

It appears that Abraham just knew *God*. The account of Abraham's faith given in Hebrews 11 says that he knew God had promised the blessings would come through

Isaac, and he reasoned that God could raise the dead. Abraham was willing to offer his son's life because He believed God could bring him back to life. Abraham wasn't sure how it would be done, but he trusted God *could* do it, and he believed God *would* do it. The man of faith believed that God could and would make it right. He trusted who God was, he trusted what God had said, and he trusted that God would continue to be trustworthy. So Abraham laid his most precious possession on the altar and offered him as a sacrifice.

Trust what you believe about God, and lay your Isaac on the altar.

What a lesson for people who want to know what God wants! Trust what you believe about God, have faith in the God you have come to know, and lay your Isaac (whatever or whoever your Isaac may be) on the altar.

But we never can *prove* the delights of His love
Until *all* on the altar we lay.
For the favor He shows and the joy He bestows
Are for those who will trust and obey.

God praised Abraham because he didn't withhold his all, his "only."

During the study of Cain's offering, I talk to my fifth graders about what God wants from us. At that time the proper answer seems to be "our best." When we study Abraham's offering, we find out what God *really* wants from us is "our all." Giving to God what He wants from us is like that little story about the chicken and the pig, each of whom was asked to make a donation for a breakfast to feed the hungry. The chicken was asked to donate eggs, and the pig was asked to give ham. The chicken, being good-hearted and well-meaning, glibly agreed for both of them until the pig pointed out, "Well, that's easy for you to say. For you it's a contribution. For me it's a total commitment!" There *is* a difference. Abraham was totally committed.

Where do I stand on the contribution-to-commitment scale? I know where God stands on it. On a mountain in the region of Moriah, the future site of Jerusalem, God substituted a sacrifice for Abraham's son, his son whom he loved. Two thousand years later on that hill in Jerusalem, God would offer His Son, His only Son whom He loved, as a sacrifice substituted for me.

∾ ∾ ∾

The relationship God had with Abraham is a relationship God promises to me and to all who choose Him. God remained faithful to Abraham his whole life. Abraham died never possessing anything in the Promised Land except a burial plot. He never knew that three world religions would claim him as their founding father. He never saw the magnificent buildings in the powerful cities or the mighty armies that would serve the nation that would grow from his loins. But he saw one son born out of impossibility, he believed in the possibility of all that God promised, and he was willing to cast everything on God. Long live the father of the faithful in our hearts. Praise the producer of the chosen children of God.

But do watch out for some of his "produce"!

6 ALL MY CHILDREN

THE BIRTH OF A NATION

You will be true to Jacob, and show mercy to Abraham,
as you pledged on oath to our fathers in days long ago.

—MICAH 7:20

GENESIS 23–36

My mother used to call me her "little ray of sunshine." To this day my baby sister grits her teeth when reminded that the appellation applied to me. (Therefore, I bring it up quite often just to stimulate things!) Something inside me wants the title to mean that I am my mother's favorite, the most admired and most admirable of her three children. It's not true, and it never was, but that doesn't mean I don't wish it were so. Who wouldn't like the title of "Most Admired" or "Most Admirable" from those they love?

Unfortunately, not only was I not my parents' favorite child, I'm not my children's favorite parent! If my kids were on national television waving at a camera to thank the person who had made the greatest difference in their lives, they would be shouting, "Hi, Dad!" (I qualify only as most entertaining parent right up to the point where I go over the edge and become most tiresome or most annoying parent.) I have long known, and have grown content with the knowledge, that both my son and my daughter are enthusiastic and absolute in their admiration of their father. I completely understand. He is a uniquely impressive and commendable individual, and he would be the one I would wave to on camera as well. Besides, it took the pressure off me to be the "good" one! I could fly a little under the radar, so to speak, while engaging in some of the bonehead moves that I frequently made in parenting and in patterning good behavior. I'm glad my offspring chose their father to emulate. At least I get half credit in the gene pool that made them that smart!

When God chose the man He would use as a pattern for what He wanted in a follower, He knew on whom to call. And no doubt about it, God chose well when He chose Abraham. He was a patriarch to be proud of, a father worth following, an ancestor to imitate. It's easy to see why the Jews throughout the New Testament and still today like to claim that relationship: children of Abraham. It's also understandable why Christians who come from his seed, the Seed that blesses all nations, claim him as their spiritual father, the father of the faithful. I even recognize the right of those who follow the teachings of Islam to claim Abraham through his loved, though "illegitimate," son Ishmael. What I worry about is that all we who claim Abraham as father usually behave less like Abraham and more like some of our other relatives who came from his family. Islamic extremists who choose not to be like Abraham but rather to behave like Ishmael, the "wild donkey of a man" whose "hand will be against everyone and everyone's hand against him, and he will live in hostility toward all his brothers," have chosen the wrong relative to relate to. As for those of us who have been called as true heirs in Christ? We also get to choose whom we model ourselves after. And remember, where we end up quite frequently depends on the "father" we've chosen to follow.

Where we end up quite frequently depends on the "father" we've chosen to follow.

MAIL ORDER

For a man who started out as one of the all-time great miracles in history, Isaac doesn't seem to have much to him. Maybe that sounds harsh, and maybe it's just because we're not told much about him, but Isaac sort of gets lost in the story somewhere between his applaudable father and his own assailable sons. Isaac appears to have been a rather passive man who preferred to keep the peace. But he also seems to have been content to let God act through him with very little questioning, whether he was being laid on an altar as a sacrifice or receiving a wife chosen for him by a servant. As much as anything, Isaac was a conduit for God's promise to Abraham's descendants to come. And at least he did what a conduit is supposed to do: he passed it on.

Most of what we know about Isaac's life—outside of a brief account of his dealings with neighbors who caused him problems and an incident when, like his father, he lied about his wife to save his own neck—is told in two stories. The first one involves finding a wife for a cherished son.

Sometime after Sarah died and was buried in the only piece of land the patriarch ever owned, Abraham recognized that his son needed a wife, and he set about finding one for him. Wanting Isaac to remain in Canaan but not wanting him to marry a Canaanite woman (with very good reason), Abraham sent a faithful servant back to the place where he was called by God and told the servant to bring back a relative for Isaac to marry. True to his nature, Abraham chose the servant well, and with the servant Eliezer being true to Abraham and to God's will, the servant also did well. He took a long trip back to the old country, pulled up to a local watering spot there, and asked for God's guidance in finding the right girl. And "before he had finished praying," God led Isaac's future wife, Rebekah, right to the servant. Isn't God great!

When Eliezer was convinced that Rebekah was the answer he had sought from God, the servant presented her with the gifts he had brought from Abraham—two gold bracelets and a gold nose ring. Personally, I'm not too sure I like the idea of a nose ring. Aren't those for oxen and bulls and other stubborn animals that need a little sterner direction? But in Rebekah's case, considering what is going to happen a little later in their lives, perhaps Isaac should have used that nose ring on her!

There is one interesting thing about the bracelets and ring the servant brought. When Rebekah ran home to tell her family about the encounter at the well and the stranger she had invited to spend the night with them, her brother, Laban, became a one-man Welcome Wagon for Abraham's servant. "As soon as he had seen the nose ring, and the bracelets on his sister's arms, and had heard Rebekah tell what the man said to her," Laban hurried out and invited the servant in. That seems harmless . . . unless you are familiar with Laban and know where future encounters with him will lead. The sight of the gold made him eager to hear where the servant had come from and what he wanted with his sister. His hopes were probably fulfilled when he found out that the servant had come from their relative Abraham, who had gone off and done quite well for himself.

Whatever the motivation, whether Rebekah's family was happy to find her a godly husband or just a good catch, they allowed her to join a caravan of strangers for a four-hundred-mile trip to a new land and a new life. And when Isaac met Rebekah and heard the story of her being chosen by God, he took her as his wife, and then he fell in love with her. So far, so good!

Actually the union of Isaac and Rebekah demonstrated quite a bit of faith. The servant counted on God to choose for him, and he believed and worshiped God when the Lord provided. Rebekah, believing she had been chosen by God, hopped on the back of a camel and went off to meet her new husband, a total stranger who, it appeared, had been chosen for her as well. And Isaac, accepting the servant's story about Rebekah being chosen by God, chose to take her as his wife. It was almost a fairy tale, except most real stories don't end with the glass slipper or the magic kiss. And so it would be with Isaac and Rebekah.

MALE ORDER

Isaac, whose birth and childhood were a miracle and whose life as an adult was marked primarily by being a peacemaker, found himself in pretty turbulent times when he entered the next stage of his life: fatherhood. Even the prophecy concerning the children who waited within his wife's body gave a clue that he wasn't always going to be able to keep the peace. The Lord told Rebekah that within her womb were two nations and two peoples, that one would be stronger than the other, and that the older would serve the younger. Now the part about the older serving the younger wasn't "right" by law, but it would be right by God. God didn't choose the younger because he deserved it. He chose him because He chose him, and planned to use the "wrong" son to accomplish His righteous plan.

When the two boys were born, life in Isaac's house got much more colorful. One boy was born red, and the other would prove to be vivid as well. Esau, which may mean "hairy," given that he was born with a "whole body like a hairy garment," was also called Edom, which definitely means "red," and he was also born red. Is it any wonder that he spent most of his time alone out in the country? And, to top it off, he was also unfortunate enough to be born first, which was usually a good thing, except in his case. When Esau was born, his younger brother was holding on to his heel and likewise to the prophecy that the older son would serve the younger. Esau's twin brother was named Jacob, meaning literally "he grasps the heel" (how creative!) and figuratively—and ultimately truly—"he deceives." The younger brother came out as a grasping individual, but it would take him many years to grasp what his purpose was in God's plan.

Esau and Jacob grew up as differently as their births indicated. Esau was a man's man, a skillful hunter who stayed out in the country doing manly things. He was Isaac's favorite, which shows that fathers who want their sons to be jocks are nothing new. Also, Isaac loved the taste of wild game, which the great red hunter would bring home. Jacob, on the other hand, was quiet and stayed pretty close to home and was something of a mama's boy. Based on appearance alone, the prophecy about the boys' places in life didn't look all that accurate. Ah, but beware the still waters that run deep and the quiet pup that jumps up and bites you when you least expect it! The time would come when everything would be put to the test, and the younger brother would show what he was made of. Jacob definitely would live up to his name and the prophecy concerning his destiny.

One day, Esau arrived home in the camp after a hunting trip, and he was famished. Jacob, the stay-at-home domestic son, had cooked up a pot of stew that enticed the manly man into a quick decision he would come to regret. When Esau reached for instant gratification to assuage his immediate hunger, claiming he would die anyway if he didn't eat, Jacob demanded a payment that would impact his long-term plan. Do you think this was a spur-of-the-moment idea by the younger brother? It's possible. Perhaps Jacob was tending to domestic business, the situation just arose, and his prophesied nature overwhelmed him. Or maybe it wasn't that innocent. Being his mother's favorite, Jacob had no doubt heard from her own lips the prophecy God had given her, and he believed he was destined for bigger things. He had observed his brother's habits and had probably calculated his weaknesses, so Jacob could have been looking for the right opportunity. Jacob knew Esau came home from his trips hungry, and he possibly thought that Esau was the stereotypical empty-headed jock who didn't really value that which meant a great deal to Jacob. It's possible that Jacob cooked a fragrant pot of stew every day in anticipation of just such an opening. But whatever the circumstances leading up to this encounter, Jacob made the first move that would propel him right into God's hands.

For a chunk of bread and a bowl of stew, Esau traded his birthright—the right to a double portion of the inheritance and the right to assume the leadership of the family upon his father's passing. It was a right reserved for the firstborn son, unless God made something else right. We Americans, who are big on what is right and what our rights are, have a hard time thinking much anything right happened that day. But that little exchange between the brothers was nothing compared to what happened next.

BLESS YOU!

Late in Isaac's life (and he had actually started late in life, marrying at forty and becoming a father at sixty), he realized his time was drawing to a close and there were things he needed to do before he died. He wanted to bless his older and favorite son with the special blessing that was a cherished custom in families of that time. The birthright was usually confirmed at the time, and the father passed on his blessing for the son's future. In the case of Isaac's sons, the blessing involved something especially important. From Abraham through Isaac had passed a special blessing direct from God, a blessing not only for them but for all who would come after them. The unique covenant with God was to pass down through Isaac to his son. A great deal was riding on *this* particular blessing.

The story of what happened with Isaac's blessing is so familiar that I usually let one of my students tell it. Most fifth graders remember how blind Isaac blessed the "wrong" heir with the help of an ambitious, protective mother, a grasping son, and some strategically placed goatskins. Nobody behaved right in this scenario, except maybe Esau, who didn't happen to be there. Isaac had "forgotten" the prophecy concerning his sons. Rebekah was sure God had forgotten and obviously needed help in the matter. And the grasper? Well, Jacob was eager to grab the blessing and birthright, whatever it took.

When Esau entered the scene for his expected blessing, he and his father realized they had been hoodwinked, bamboozled, and definitely outwitted. Isaac couldn't undo the blessing he had given to Jacob. The sold birthright was made legal by the stolen blessing, so it all officially belonged to Jacob, and Esau was left with leftovers. Although it seemed like a total victory for Jacob and his doting mother, Rebekah, no one was going to come out unscathed in this deal.

The price Esau paid for having "despised" his birthright is clear: he lost it all. What is really sad is that he didn't even realize how much he had lost.

The price Isaac paid is less noticeable, but he lost too. His favorite son, the one he wanted to bless above the younger, was sentenced to a life away from the Lord's riches and under the dominion of his newly enriched brother. And probably less visible to him, Isaac lost something vital. He performed God's will, but he did it without choosing to. That makes me sad. Isaac had lived most of his life watching his father make the right choices and heed God's voice (Isaac was seventy-five years old when Abraham died), yet when the time came for Isaac to remember God's words and to follow God's will for his sons, he had forgotten God's words and wrongly followed his own will. He had an opportunity to trumpet God and His plan. But instead, Isaac missed his chance to be great among the faithful. That stands as a warning to us. God's will is going to be done. We get to choose whether we're accidental participants or willing partners. Esau and Isaac lost.

God's will is going to be done. We get to choose whether we're accidental participants or willing partners.

But Rebekah and Jacob didn't completely win. The mother, who was so ambitious for Jacob that she would ensure God carried out His will for her son, after all this was over would never see her son again. I'm sure she felt justified in what she did. She was doing God's will. In fact, she was doing it *for* Him just in case He couldn't pull it off on His own!

I'm certainly glad it would never occur to me to try to help God out. I'm glad that I'm always so patient with God's timing, that I'm never spurred by a desire to help Him along with things that need to be done! I have a good friend who had to absorb some pretty hard blows in her early life yet kept on trying to learn the lessons and to pass them along to other people who needed help. In fact, she chose to become a Christian counselor. But one circumstance was particularly devastating, and she felt forced to tell God, "If I keep having all these things happen, I don't know if I'm going to be able to keep helping You." She said, "Don't you know that caused a panic in heaven! Don't you know the Lord called all His angels together and said, 'What are we going to do? Glenda isn't going to help us anymore!'" I love that story, and I love her for telling it. It illustrates how ignorant (bordering on arrogant) we can be when we feel like God may need our help to get His good stuff done.

Rebekah may have had good intentions. She overheard her husband planning to subvert God's will, and she acted to make sure that didn't happen. But I'm not convinced her motives were all that pure since she seemed more concerned with Jacob's inheritance in *Isaac's* will rather than with *God's* will. And I'm quite certain her methods were underhanded and meanspirited. She proved herself a wonderful role model for deceitfulness, and her son, the deceiver by name and deed, proved a quick study.

Jacob *took* what God meant to *give* him. With his actions he unwittingly began a life that would be marked for many years by deceit, alienation, loss, and strife.

There were no winners in this enterprise. Unless you count God, that is.

God's will was done in the matter of Esau and Jacob. God's blessing through the family of Abraham was passed on to the one He intended. His plan for the salvation of the world would go through the man He chose. The chosen Jacob would be changed in the course of his history with God. And that may be why he was chosen. Why *would* God choose a man like Jacob to accomplish His good and perfect will? Well, for one thing, Jacob wanted what God was offering. Esau "despised" his birthright, we're told. He traded it for a bowl of stew. He just didn't care that much about it. God won't force us to *care* about something. It's that heart thing again. It's that free will thing He established in the beginning. I would like to make my own children love God. I would like to make my fifth-grade students love God. But I can't. All I can do is tell them why they should love God. That is, in a nutshell, what I try to teach my class. All God will do is show us and tell us why we *should* love Him. But God, by His decision to give us the freedom to choose what we love, won't make us love Him. He calls us. He woos us. Sometimes He tests us. And above all things, God intensely desires for us to love Him, but He will not make us love Him. God didn't make Esau value his birthright. But God did take Jacob, who yearned for it, who valued it above his own integrity, and God would channel that yearning for His purpose.

What a mess God's little family found itself in! Isaac thought he was dying (turns out he was really wrong about that). Esau was "consoling himself with the thought of killing" Jacob (what a great phrase!). And Rebekah realized that the only way to save Jacob, the now chosen one, was to send him away until Esau's anger subsided and he "forgot" what had been done to him. Not wanting Jacob vulnerable to Esau or the influences of Canaan, Isaac and Rebekah agreed he should go to the home of her brother Laban in the old country. So she packed him up and sent him off. And Jacob ran for his life . . . in more ways than one.

DESTINY'S CHILD

Jacob ran away from home. He ran away from his brother, Esau. He ran away from everything he knew. And while running away, he ran toward God. He didn't know it. He didn't mean to. But as Jacob ran, God was waiting for him.

Jacob ran all day, and then because it got dark, he lay down to sleep, and as he slept, he dreamed. He dreamed of a stairway that rested on the earth and reached into the heavens, and on the stairway was two-way traffic between heaven and earth. God was there, as if He had come down to show the way into His presence, and He introduced Himself to Jacob: "I am the LORD, the God of your father Abraham and the God of Isaac." And then He gave Jacob that for which he had been chosen: the blessing, the covenant promise made with Abraham and passed down through Isaac, the promise of land and greatness, and the promise of a blessing for the world. And He promised Jacob His presence: "I am with you and will watch over you wherever you go, and I will bring you back to this land. I will not leave you until I have done what I have promised you."

God likes to give His children two important things when He calls them into His service: help for the present and hope for the future. Jacob thought he was alone in the world. He had run from everything he had known and depended on. But God assured Jacob of His presence and promised that His presence would remain with him. Jacob met the God who wanted to be not just the God of his grandfather and father but his own God, forever. And Jacob vowed to accept the Lord as his God. God wasn't going to give Jacob credit just for being a descendant of Abraham. God has no grandchildren, only children, each in a personal relationship with Him.

God likes to give His children two important things—help for the present and hope for the future.

So Jacob chose God, who had chosen him. He said, "Surely the LORD is in this place, and I was not aware of it. How awesome is this place! This is none other than the house of God; this is the gate of heaven." Jacob declared his personal allegiance to God and declared his stone pillow a pillar in the place he named Bethel, meaning "house of God." Then he resumed his journey, and whether or not he recognized it at the time, the "grasper" finally started down the road that would eventually lead him to grasp what God had in mind for him.

It's too bad it would take him most of his life to get where he was going. Like everyone who begins a journey toward, and even with, God, Jacob was carrying quite a bit of baggage, and I don't mean a suitcase. It's hard to leave behind one's past, and it's even harder to leave behind one's basic nature. Jacob was about to get a dose of his own medicine, for when the deceiver met his uncle Laban, he met his match.

As soon as Jacob arrived in the vicinity of Haran, the homeland of his relatives, he began searching for the home of his mother's brother. His first glimpse of a relative was all it took to convince himself he had come to the right place. When the fair Rachel, "lovely in form, and beautiful," batted her eyes in his direction, he was well and truly lost. He introduced himself with a macho act of rolling away a large stone from the mouth of a well and then got in touch with his feminine side by weeping aloud when he told her who he was. He was indeed a renaissance man, and Rachel seemed as smitten with him as he was with her. Jacob was admitted into his mother's family and immediately went to work for his uncle Laban. When asked what he wanted as a wage for his work, Jacob agreed it would be fair to give seven years of labor for the hand of the comely Rachel. Both Laban and Jacob thought they had made the deal of the century.

You've Got Males

The years flew by as if they were days, and Jacob worked joyfully in anticipation of wedding his beloved. Laban was doing a little anticipating of his own. He was anticipating unloading something of a liability.

It seems Laban had two daughters: the lovely Rachel and an older daughter named Leah. It wasn't enough that she was older and had no prospects for marriage, but Leah is described as having "weak eyes." What do you reckon that means? She wore Coke-bottle lenses? She couldn't go outside because the sun hurt her eyes, so she was a white, molelike creature living in the dark? Or maybe she was so homely it hurt the eyes of anyone who looked at her. Whatever it means, Leah wasn't as desirable as Rachel, but her father decided to help her out a little and help himself out in the process.

Laban proved he was the master of the game in which both Jacob and his mother excelled. He deceived the deceiver. For Jacob's wedding Laban gave a feast. Either there was a whole lot of drinking at the bachelor party, or brides were heavily veiled in that Middle Eastern world, because the next morning, after having slept with his new wife, Jacob woke up, and his eyes started burning. Instead of Rachel, there was Leah, his new, legal wife. When Jacob demanded to know what had been done, Laban said something like, "Oh, didn't I tell you that it's not our custom to marry off the younger sister before the older? I could have sworn I mentioned that. Well, I'm sorry about the misunderstanding. Let's make another deal." So Jacob made a deal, although I'm not sure he got a bargain.

The deceiver had been deceived. How did that happen? How could the master of duplicity be the victim of such double-dealing? Jacob received what his own father and brother had received from him: he had been hoodwinked, bamboozled, and definitely outwitted.

The old saying applies here: "Oh what a tangled web we weave when first we practice to deceive." Did Jacob have a clue how tangled everything was going to get? He'd fled a home torn by favoritism, deceit, and strife, but he fell right into the patterns of the past. He became the head of a home that would make Jerry Springer blanch, a family that could define "dysfunctional," a group that throughout its history would be shredded by the same things that had torn up Jacob's boyhood home. Many years ago I read an apt description of the long-term effects of bad choices: they have a "long leg and a hard foot." In the case of Jacob's family, the effects of discord would indeed be long and hard, and they would deal some jarring kicks.

Bad choices have a "long leg and a hard foot."

Jacob was married to Leah, but he loved Rachel. And in return for giving Leah one week of wedded bliss and agreeing to work *another* seven years, Jacob got to marry Rachel also. And then things really got interesting, soap-opera interesting: two wives, two handmaidens, and one man servicing them all. I understand it is from this example that Muslims believe it is okay to have four wives. Which story did they read that convinced them this was a good idea? A good idea it may not have been, but it certainly makes for a "good" story!

"When the Lord saw that Leah was not loved," He stepped into her life and gave her the ability to be fruitful, while making the much-loved Rachel barren. (I really love the picture of the Lord choosing to love Leah when her husband could not or would not.) Leah began to produce sons, hoping to win her husband's love. Rachel, secure in her husband's love but jealously competing with her sister, tried to produce sons in her own way. The story flies as Leah had four sons and Rachel procured two sons with the help of her handmaiden. Leah, not to be outdone, appropriated two sons through her handmaiden. Then Rachel, with a strong desire for some of Leah's mandrakes (medicine for menstrual pain? tension headache?), bargained with Leah, and Leah "hired" Jacob and produced two more sons and a daughter. Whew! Jacob kept up quite a schedule, working in the fields by day and the tents by night.

We don't know if Jacob got more than temporary pleasure from his activities, but we do know he had two women dealing with more permanent miseries. One woman had lots of children but not the love of her husband, which she desperately wanted. The other woman had the love of her husband but no children, which she desperately wanted. No one was happy in this family. And it was going to get worse.

Finally, as a balm to Rachel's spirit, to the everlasting joy of her husband and for the far-reaching good of God's chosen children, God "remembered" Rachel. He opened her barren womb, and she became the mother of the golden boy, Joseph. I doubt many births have been more welcomed. At last great love produced one who would become the recipient of great love and ultimately the dispenser of great love. This child was truly destined for greatness. In the annals of great and good men, Joseph would stand out as one of the greatest and best. But before God would work it out for good, man would do his best to work up some bad.

Shortly after Joseph's birth and maybe because of it, Jacob decided it was time to leave Laban's home and return to his homeland with his family and everything that rightfully belonged to him. Laban wasn't eager to lose his daughters, grandchildren, and a very productive son-in-law/laborer. The two deceivers went at each other for a while, mixing it up with streaked, spotted, and speckled goats and the breeding thereof. After some time, with the admitted help of the Lord, Jacob bested Laban in the contest, packed up his family and all his considerable possessions and flocks, and sneaked out of town. Laban pursued and confronted him, and ultimately the two deceivers made a covenant to end the conflict between them.

Then, speaking of conflict, Jacob headed home to meet his brother, Esau.

JAKE'S NOT NIMBLE, JAKE'S NOT QUICK, JACOB'S LEANING ON HIS WALKING STICK

Jacob began his long journey back to the home he had left in fear and haste. But to get home, he knew he would have to go past his brother, in fact, through his brother. Jacob would come face to face with the man he had cheated of all that belonged to him, the man who had vowed to kill him as soon as their father died, and Jacob was afraid.

He made preparations to protect his family and selected gifts to appease Esau, and then Jacob prayed. He prayed for God's protection, humbly admitting he was undeserving of it, and he called upon God's covenant promise of prosperity and longevity for his descendants. Then he rested.

I'm not sure there was any way Jacob could have prepared for what happened next. He had another meeting with God! It appears that God liked to meet Jacob coming and going. This time God met him in a wrestling match that lasted all night. God started it, but Jacob insisted it not end until God blessed him.

God finally caused Jacob to submit by wrenching his hip socket, and from that day on, Jacob would limp and have to lean on something in order to support himself. In fact, in Hebrews 11, the roll call of the faithful, we are told that when Jacob was dying, he worshiped as he leaned on the top of his staff. The changed man would never again be able to completely depend on his own strength but would be forced to lean on God. Since Jacob was a shepherd by occupation, I wonder if he recognized the significance of his lameness. When a sheep was prone to wandering, thus putting itself in danger, shepherds of old sometimes resorted to breaking the sheep's leg and splinting it, thus forcing the sheep to stay right by the shepherd for help in making its way. By the time the leg healed, the sheep was in the habit of remaining close to the shepherd and never wandered again. Sometimes, in our struggles with God, He breaks us down to rebuild us and make us better.

Sometimes, in our struggles with God, He breaks us down to rebuild us and make us better.

DADDY'S HOME

That night, after Jacob's submission, God changed his name and confirmed his destiny. The Lord named him "Israel," which translates "struggles with God." The old man went from "Jacob," a man who definitely struggled with men, to "Israel," a man who struggled with God. Whether it meant that he would struggle against God or that any of his future struggles would have God's help, it preaches either way. Jacob/Israel would become the father of a nation that would proudly bear the name Israel, and the nation would continue to struggle *with* God even when God offered to struggle *for* them.

Then fresh from his meeting with God, Jacob faced Esau. Actually, that's probably a good time to face a potentially angry brother or sister: when we're fresh from being with God. It provides us the strength we will undoubtedly need to deal with another flawed human. Significantly, Jacob's meeting with Esau was not what he had feared, and in fact it was a relief and a blessing as he met a brother who welcomed him home. Esau forgave Jacob for stealing his "rightful" riches, because he had become rich in his own right. Perhaps proving that he hadn't valued his birthright and thus a place in God's plan, Esau seemed happy to relinquish God's richness for his own. (Be careful before you decide that this is the relative you want to emulate. Being rich and being enriched are frequently two completely different things.)

Jacob was able to reconcile with his father as well. He introduced Isaac to the children who were going to become the nation God had promised to Isaac and to Abraham before him. Things looked pretty good in general. Unfortunately for Jacob and his family, there was still a piper to be paid.

A short time after returning to his homeland, Jacob lost his dearly loved Rachel during the birth of his youngest son, Benjamin. One might hope Jacob would take the opportunity to establish a closer bond with Leah and her children, but it didn't happen. Jacob's life would remain closely entangled with the cherished Rachel through her sons. His children by Leah and the handmaidens would go largely unloved, and they would know it. Jacob, whose early life had been deeply marked by parents who played favorites, would show great favoritism toward Rachel's sons.

It would be one of his costlier mistakes.

7 DREAM A LITTLE DREAM

JOSEPH

And who knows but that you have come to royal position
for such a time as this?

—ESTHER 4:14

GENESIS 37–50

As a kid, I frequently had visions of what I wanted to look like, what I wanted to be like, how I wanted to live when I grew up. No one in my family dreamed my dreams, but it never deterred me from dreaming them. For instance, I always wanted long hair, and when my head would produce only sparse twigs that looked much better short, my mother would keep my hair cropped, and I would manufacture a ponytail out of scarves and other assorted flowing things. In my dreams I was beautiful and life was wonderful . . . except for another unfilled longing. Every night for a year I prayed for a horse, and every morning when I looked out my bedroom window, I was truly surprised when my backyard contained only the debris that had blown in on the West Texas wind. To the relief of my parents, I finally contented myself by riding a mop (with a luxurious "mane") or letting my sister ride me. It took me a few years to give up my deepest desire to be adopted by Roy Rogers, but gradually I learned to live within the constraints of my parents' home. As for my dream house, it would have been full of dogs and cats, but I certainly dreamed that one myself since my parents weren't much on having pets. Finally in desperation, I had to become my own dog! During that phase I assumed the job of barking at the neighbors through the screen door. Okay, now I just sound nuts. But I did have dreams! Every family needs a dreamer, don't you think?

Jacob's family produced one such dreamer. His dreams must have seemed as out of reach and as out of touch with reality to his family as mine appeared to those who heard my dreams. The difference in my dreams and Joseph's, though, was that while my dreams came from a powerful imagination, his came from a powerful God.

Jacob was the father of lots of sons. It should have been his great blessing as a Hebrew father. It turned out though to be something of a mixed blessing. The first ten sons had grown up in a household with squabbling women making most of the decisions and a gun-shy husband just trying to stay out of harm's way. They'd witnessed their grandfather and their father jockeying for fiscal position and trying to outmaneuver each other. None of the adults in these scenarios appears to have had much regard for the effect on tender young minds and hearts. What the boys saw as they grew up was jealousy, deceit, grasping for one's share, resentment of one's lot in life, and a rather unhappy, unsatisfactory home life. In that atmosphere they learned about family values. There was no way they would come out unscathed. As it turned out, they all got pretty "scathed." And then Joseph was born.

When the dearly loved Rachel gave birth to her first son, it was cause for great celebration, at least in one household. Jacob reveled in Joseph as the offspring of his great and true love for Rachel, and by his treatment of Joseph, Jacob obviously considered him his true firstborn son. Benjamin, the son born when Rachel died in childbirth, just after the return home, was likewise special to his father, but without question Joseph was the favorite.

He had learned the futility of fighting what God wanted and the benefits of becoming who He needed.

Joseph also benefited by growing up with a "different" father than the ten older boys. The older brothers had fashioned themselves after the old Jacob. But the Jacob who returned to live in Canaan had wrestled with God and had been changed into a man who leaned on God. He had learned the futility of fighting what God wanted and the benefits of becoming who He needed. He must have frequently spoken the name of God in worship, because Joseph's life would show that he had developed (from his father?) a deep trust in who God is and what God wants from believers. We'll also see that Joseph knew about the prophecies concerning God's people. *Someone* must have taught him. But what that someone taught the other ten, well, that was a little different, and it would cause much heartache for everyone concerned.

THE COLOR OF CONFLICT

Our first glimpse of Joseph in Genesis 37 is of a young man we, too, might have felt like smacking had we been his siblings. He was seventeen years old, secure in his father's love, which his brothers were not, and something of a tattletale, which his brothers resented.

But the problems really started with the coat. Anyone who has ever heard of Joseph knows about his coat of many colors or his "Amazing Technicolor Dreamcoat," a "richly ornamented robe." Whatever it looked like, it certainly looked like favoritism. In fact the first mention of the coat comes in a paragraph that starts with "Now Israel [Jacob] loved Joseph more than any of his other sons" and ends with the fact that his brothers "hated him and could not speak a kind word to him." Whether it was the kind of coat that traditionally marked its wearer as the firstborn son or as royalty, the coat made Joseph a marked man.

"When his brothers *saw* that their father loved him more than any of them, they hated him." No doubt they knew Joseph was closer to their father than they were. They had known Rachel and how much Jacob loved her, and maybe they even understood that Jacob would favor Joseph a little. But the coat apparently was an in-your-face admission that Joseph was really the *only* son who mattered to Jacob. I have a hard time not feeling sorry for the brothers. What they did to Joseph and Jacob later on was heinous and definitely wrong, but these young men acted out of pain and rejection by a father who never loved them as they deserved. Yeah, I'm pretty sure the coat started it. Throw in the dreams, and you might as well throw in a stick of dynamite.

After having some weird dreams, Joseph went looking for his brothers to tell them what he'd dreamed. He was probably wearing the coat while he talked. Since they were already predisposed to resent anything he said, the brothers were less than pleased with what Joseph told them. In the two dreams, the brothers' sheaves bowed low before Joseph's sheaf, which rose and stood upright, and the sun and moon and eleven stars bowed down to Joseph. As a result of Joseph's dreams, "they hated him all the more." The brothers were indignant at Joseph's audacity. Even Jacob rebuked his young son when he learned that he himself had bowed before Joseph in the dream. But while the brothers were ruled by their hatred and jealousy, Jacob "kept the matter in mind." It was probably like Mary, who "pondered . . . in her heart" all the things she heard about the new baby Jesus. In both instances, parents received veiled hints of what was to come in the life of their child.

Finally, in one fateful day, everything fell together for the ten brothers to right a few wrongs. They had everything they needed to avenge themselves against both Joseph and Jacob (and to be convicted in a court of law): the means, the motive, and the opportunity to commit a terrible crime.

The opportunity just seemed to present itself. Jacob sent Joseph out into the country to look for his brothers and to check on their welfare while they were grazing the flock in greener pastures. If being far removed from Jacob's watchful eye would help in the brothers' opportunity to act out their displeasure, that was covered. The group had traveled quite a distance from home by the time Joseph found them. He tracked the group about forty miles from home to Shechem and then another several miles before he located them in Dothan. Hints of further opportunity: Dothan appears to have been on a major trade route to Egypt. What is one supposed to do if an opportunity just arises?

To the brothers' way of thinking, they had a good motive for getting rid of the one who obviously stood between them and their father's favor. Jealousy, envy, resentment, hatred that had grown with every act of favoritism shown—combined, it was a deadly mix. Then throw in a little mob mentality. And don't forget the coat! The little dreamer came sauntering up to his older brothers wearing that infamous coat. What happened next the brothers probably figured Joseph had coming to him.

There was opportunity, there was motive to spare, and the means presented itself with a dry hole in the desert. Like a rebellious rabble, the ten resolved to kill their younger brother and discard his body in the well (after gleefully removing the hated coat). A cooler head prevailed when Reuben urged his brothers not to kill Joseph but rather to let him die in the well. We're told that Reuben intended to rescue Joseph later but never got the opportunity, because the other brothers, led by Judah, decided to sell Joseph instead. Oh, that's much better. There would be no gain in killing him, and they could make a little money by selling him as a slave. Then they wouldn't be so guilty either.

So Joseph was dragged out of the pit and sold to a caravan of Ishmaelites on the way to Egypt. What great irony. The descendants of the illegitimate, sold-out son of Abraham bought a descendant of the true heir. I love the way God works! (Mentioned almost interchangeably with the Ishmaelites are the Midianites, other descendants of Abraham through a woman named Keturah, a probable concubine or "second wife" taken after Sarah's death. Perhaps the displaced offspring of Abraham joined together in their displacement.) It appears that Joseph's close relatives sold him to his distant relatives, which would land him in the distant land of Egypt. And now the distance between Joseph and his family would be spanned only by an act of God.

> *The distance between Joseph and his family would be spanned only by an act of God.*

Immediately after selling Joseph, his brothers began to try to cover themselves. They never expected to see their brother again, so they could tell Jacob anything they wanted. They decided that rather than make up a story and therefore be liars (heaven forbid!), they would let the precious coat tell the story to their father. The brothers dipped Joseph's tattered coat in goat's blood, took it to Jacob, and let him discern for himself that his beloved son had met a violent end in the jaws of a ferocious animal. Jacob mourned inconsolably for his son. Little did he know that God had chosen to use the "death" of Joseph to give life to the rest of his family.

WALK LIKE AN EGYPTIAN

Joseph was taken from his homeland to a foreign country—and from being the cherished son of a wealthy man to being the impoverished slave of a mighty man. But there is a phrase that recurs several times in the story of Joseph's life in Egypt: "the LORD was with Joseph." What happened next, no person could have predicted—not Joseph, not Joseph's father, and certainly not Joseph's brothers. But it was no surprise to God. God would use what the brothers meant for harm to accomplish His good purposes with His people.

God was on the move, and the movement for Joseph would be swift and upward. From a lowly slave, Joseph became the valued head of the household of Potiphar, one of Pharaoh's officials. But the boss's wife became warm for his form. (He must have taken after his mother since, in a book that gives few physical descriptions of its many people, both were described as beautiful in face and body.) Joseph continually rejected Mrs. Potiphar's advances out of faithfulness to both his Lord God and to his master, so she falsely accused him of molesting her and he was thrown into prison. The place "happened" to house the prisoners of the king himself, and true to his pattern and because the Lord was with him (again and continuously), Joseph was soon in charge of the prison.

God would use what the brothers meant for harm to accomplish His good purposes with His people.

When some of the king's own servants were thrown into "Joseph's" prison, he ministered to them and, through God, interpreted their dreams, which came to pass just as foretold. Finally Joseph came to the attention of the king himself when Pharaoh had a dream that needed interpreting. Joseph went before the number-one man in the number-one country of the world and told him what his dream meant: that Egypt would have a time of abundance followed by a grueling famine and that Pharaoh would need a discerning and wise man to prepare the nation to survive. Pharaoh discerned that no one was wiser than Joseph, so he put him in charge.

Joseph was thirty years old when he became the second most powerful man in the most powerful nation in the world. It had taken him thirteen years to go from number-one son to number-two Egyptian. It may not have seemed brief to Joseph, but it's amazing to me how expeditiously God moved in Joseph's life in Egypt. Joseph acknowledged it was God who was moving him along, but God's next moves would be a really moving experience, for his children and Egypt!

REUNITED AND IT FEELS SO GOOD

Soon the forecasted famine that enveloped Egypt likewise afflicted the rest of the world, including Canaan, where Joseph's family lived. When Jacob learned grain could be purchased in Egypt, he sent his ten older sons to buy food. But being Jacob, who still cherished the sons of Rachel above his other sons, he kept Benjamin at home to protect him from any possible harm.

So one day, as Joseph stood in the granary of Egypt, ten sheaves came in and bowed before the big sheaf himself! Joseph recognized his brothers, though they didn't see in the face of the governor of Egypt any resemblance to the younger brother they had so callously cast off thirteen years before. Joseph could have chosen to repay them in kind, but he didn't. He was truly one of God's good guys. Instead of getting rid of his brothers, Joseph maneuvered them into bringing Benjamin to Egypt. After some time and some crafty moves during several encounters, he finally revealed himself as their brother. Joseph wept, even wailed, as he told them who he was and asked about the welfare of his father. And the brothers were overjoyed too, right? Not quite! They were absolutely stunned into silence and terrified into immobility. Surely their lives flashed before their eyes at the realization of what this encounter might mean.

But Joseph was totally surrendered to the God who had so personally and perfectly directed his life to this point. He, with total conviction and sincerity, absolved his brothers of any responsibility for where he had ended up. He told them that God's moves, not theirs, had directed his life. In fact, he told them that God had sent him away to Egypt *so* they would all be saved. Joseph recognized that God had made him lord over all Egypt for a reason. But my favorite thing he told his brothers was something even he might not have fully understood: God had sent Joseph ahead to preserve a remnant on earth and to save their lives "by a great deliverance"! I think Joseph would have been thrilled if he had known what that really meant, what God was ultimately planning to do with His children who had come to Egypt.

He was a man who was convicted that God's plan and God's rule superseded his own needs and his own life.

While being told only part of God's plan, yet grasping much of God's heart, Joseph was willing to be used by God for the well-being of the rest of His children. Joseph was not the Seed-bearer in the line of Abraham. Jesus's line would be traced through Judah (a son of Leah, which touches my heart). But Joseph would protect the line that carried the Seed. He was a planner who knew he had a place in God's plan. He was a ruler who was submitted to God's rule. And he was a man who was convicted that God's plan and God's rule superseded his own needs and his own life. So Joseph forgave his brothers for their actions. Even though they intended to harm him, God "intended it for good." The great God of Israel had even used Joseph's *unwilling* brothers to accomplish His will and plan. God sent Joseph to Egypt ahead of his brothers, planning for them to come, so He could save His children from famine but mostly so he could deliver them from far more than famine. Egypt would become an incubator for God's Seed.

Could Joseph have known God's plans? When God confirmed His covenant with Abraham, He told him, "Know for certain that your descendants will be strangers in a country not their own, and they will be enslaved and mistreated four hundred years. But I will punish the nation they serve as slaves, and afterward they will come out with great possessions." From the beginning of time, God has wanted His people to understand who He is and to believe what He will do for those who are His. Abraham had heard God's promise, and Joseph had believed it. Neither could know exactly what God would do in the future of His people, but each knew God held His people's future in His perfect plan.

After Joseph reconciled with his brothers, he sent for his father to join them all in Egypt. With great joy Jacob set out on his journey to see his son. And, as often happened when Jacob journeyed, he had a meeting with God on the way. This time, rather than appearing to him in a grand vision or engaging him in a wrestling match, God simply spoke to Jacob. Though simple, the message was of great import: "I am God, the God of your father. Do not be afraid to go down to Egypt, for I will make you into a great nation there. I will go down to Egypt with you, and I will surely bring you back again." And He would.

Jacob joined his beloved Joseph and spent seventeen years living well in Egypt. Before he died there, he passed on the family blessing to Judah and gave a special blessing to Joseph's younger son, Ephraim. (These two tribes of Israel would eventually contend for supremacy with each other—Rehoboam vs. Jeroboam—and produce many of the strong leading men of Israel, thus reinforcing the woes of favoritism and continuing the struggle of the brothers.) When Jacob died, his body was carried back to Canaan for burial, and he was laid to rest with Abraham and Sarah, Isaac and Rebekah . . . and Leah. Jacob's own sons plus Joseph's two sons would become the twelve tribes of Israel, a great nation under God.

As the book of Genesis closes, the little family of God, His chosen ones, had found a dwelling place in a foreign land. The family of Abraham, divinely designed to become God's chosen nation, would remain in Egypt until God himself would go down there to deliver them and take them home.

8   Smooth Moves

God Calls His People Out of Egypt

See, the Lord rides on a swift cloud and is coming to Egypt.

—Isaiah 19:1

Exodus 1:1–14:12

Since I am quite often unsure of what I am about, it's with great comfort that I embrace the knowledge that God has always known what He is about. Moreover, He has always known what mankind would be, and He has always known what mankind would need. Even with humanity's tendencies to do, think, and feel everything wrong, God has been true to His love for humans. He is faithful to save us in spite of us.

Remember, however, that the children of Israel didn't have the privilege of turning the page in the Bible to see how God was working. We're talking about decades, sometimes centuries, passing between God's revelations. And we're talking about people who were not any different than you or me. There were times when God's promises seemed pretty dim. Abraham, Isaac, and Jacob—the receivers of the covenant—lived as nomads who never founded a city, let alone anything resembling a nation. They were pilgrims following God's lead, never finding yet always being led onward by the promise of greatness in a land where their descendants would settle and thrive. They were people following a dream that never seemed to

> *It is always good to be God's child, but it isn't always easy.*

come true and sometimes seemed more like a nightmare. It is always good to be God's child, but it isn't always easy.

GOD MOVES AMONG HIS PEOPLE

Genesis 46 lists the seventy members of the family Israel who settled in Egypt's "land o' Goshen" and were in high favor with the Egyptians because of the character and faithfulness of Joseph.

The book of Exodus picks up the story after more than three hundred years had passed. Jacob and Joseph had died, but their family had grown into a multitude. They had followed God's instructions for His people whenever they entered a new world, whether it was the garden, the land after the flood, or Egypt. They were fruitful, and they multiplied, and they filled the land. We're then told an important detail: "a new king, who did not know about Joseph, came to power in Egypt." It says quite a bit about Joseph that it took that many years for the Egyptians to forget who he was and what he had done for their country.

Nevertheless, the new leader of Egypt looked around and saw that his land was filled with people who did not belong in the Egyptian world. Egyptians worshiped many gods; the foreigners worshiped one. Egyptians were world-renowned architects who erected beautiful buildings in stable cities; these foreigners wandered around from pillar to post, living in the ancient equivalent of trailer parks, and were shepherds, a most detestable vocation. Egyptians were cultured and educated; the foreigners were rural rubes and, in addition, reproduced like rabbits. They were very foreign, and there were very many of them!

So the king in Egypt, fearing a possible uprising, made a few changes. He forced the descendants of Joseph's father into slave labor to control their numbers, and he forced them to build cities in an effort to contain their movement. As a result they multiplied in number and spread from the country into the cities. Oops! So the Egyptians became ruthless in their treatment of the people they called Hebrews, which may be a translation of a derogative Egyptian word *hapiru*, meaning "the dusty ones." The king even ordered the killing of the Hebrews' male children in an effort to wipe out the people. Egypt brutalized God's chosen people to prevent the *possibility* that they might revolt.

I'm sure you've heard the phrase "Let sleeping dogs lie." It's a warning about what happens when the status quo is messed with. I think when the king of Egypt began his reign of terror against God's people, he poked a sleeping dog. And with the help of a powerful Master, that snoozing beast was going to jump up and badly bite the man with the stick.

Although the Egyptians noticed that the Hebrews did not belong in Egypt, the same might not have been true of the Hebrews themselves. It appears that God's people had been content with the status quo for three hundred years. Their forebears had been wanderers; Egypt had rich grazing land for their sheep. In Canaan they had been at the mercy of any passing travelers, spread out as they were in isolated pockets across the land; Egypt offered the protection of the most powerful nation in the world to those who lived within its borders. Perhaps the Israelites were content to stay in Egypt and continue as they had for several centuries. They had no obvious plans to revolt or any burning desire to leave what appeared to be the good life.

Therefore, I am convinced it was God who put the stick in the king's hand and persuaded him to poke the sleeping dog. God did not want His people to be content in someone else's land when He had called them to a land of their own. His people needed to wake up and realize they had gone to sleep on the job. So God put a really sharp stick in the hand of a pagan king and jabbed His people into awareness. And when the injured dog began to howl, God began to work.

BABY STEPS

Eighty years before the man would be needed, a boy was born. He was born in Egypt to a family of Israelites from the tribe of Levi, born during a time of great fear because Hebrew baby boys were being slaughtered. We know little about his father, who was most likely busy being a slave, but he had a brother, a sister, and a mother, whom Bible students get to know pretty well. The Hebrew mother, Jochebed, had to take special care to assure her son's survival. For three months she hid him from his would-be killers, but when it became inevitable that he would be found as he grew, she came up with another plan. She made a tiny boat of papyrus, coated it with tar to make it waterproof, placed her baby boy inside, and hid him in the reed-protected shore of the Nile River under the watchful eye of his older sister, Miriam. Though we're told it was by faith that she hid him, it's doubtful she purposely placed him where he would be found by Pharaoh's daughter, as some suggest. Why would she assume that the daughter of the man who was killing Hebrew babies would save one, even one described as a "fine child"? Could it have been the hand of God that gave the basket a little shove in the direction of destiny?

I doubt the people involved in the early life of Moses knew where their actions would lead. When Jochebed worked to save her baby's life, she likely had no idea his destiny was to save her people's lives. While Miriam watched over him, she didn't know he would be the future shepherd who would oversee God's flock. When Pharaoh's daughter drew baby Moses out of the water and took him into her home to raise, she didn't realize he would raise a ruckus in her country that would never be equaled. No one knew that the tiny baby each took into her heart would, in time, clearly reveal the heart of God. The great God of Israel directed every phase of Moses' life, and most of the time even Moses wouldn't know where He was leading. It would take eighty years for God to train Moses and turn him into the man most consider to be God's greatest.

Moses could not grasp all that he might gain by choosing God, but he certainly knew what he would lose by not choosing Egypt.

During the first forty years of Moses' life, he received the best Egypt had to offer, compliments of Pharaoh's household. He was educated and cultured in the best way that the best country of his day could offer. Also because of God's placement, Moses' own mother was able to nurse him and enlighten him in the culture and religion of his true family.

Two worlds would clash when Moses was forced to choose the direction for his life. He would have to choose between the culture that shaped him and the God who had formed him and placed him. It would have been quite tempting to choose what Egypt offered: education and culture, tremendous wealth, and the prominence that came from being a member, likely even an heir, of the royal household. Was the choice easy? Hardly. Moses could not grasp all that he might gain by choosing God, but he certainly knew what he would lose by not choosing Egypt. (Is our choice so different today?)

Somewhere in the heart of the prince of Egypt was the knowledge that he was in reality an Israelite slave, and by faith he made his choice. Whatever it might mean for him, Moses left behind the temporary reward of the world he knew and took the first step toward a world he couldn't imagine. One day Moses went out to where his own people were and saw them being treated like slaves, and he chose sides. He killed an Egyptian who was mistreating a Hebrew. Maybe Moses was making a statement of where he stood not only to himself but to the Israelites as well: "I'm one of you guys!" The Israelites weren't exactly interested in having him join them. How were they to recognize him as one of their own? So Moses' choice of sides didn't sit well with either side. He ended up having to run for his life from the people he had rejected and from the people who had rejected him. He might have thought twice about his choice if he had seen where it would lead him.

Moses ran away from everything he had known and, like Jacob before him, ran right into God's waiting arms. At the time it's doubtful he recognized God was in total control of his life. He probably didn't think about it being God who led him into the wilderness and turned him into a shepherd. Unlike those of us who have been privileged to read the whole book, Moses had no idea that the wilderness would play such a prominent role in his life, that it would, in fact, be the backdrop for the rest of his life. Nor did he know how much he would need to learn about herding!

And to make it even more interesting, while running away from two families who had just rejected him, Moses ended up running into some of his cousins. He was taken in by a group of Midianites, those dispossessed descendants of Abraham through his "second wife." They were the people who had bought Joseph and sold him in Egypt. Don't you love the way God works? The same people who served as transport for God's people *into* Egypt would nurture the one chosen to transport them *out!*

Moses was embraced by the family of Jethro, a Midianite priest, and he married Jethro's daughter Zipporah and began his own family. Just as he had settled into his life as an Egyptian for forty years, so Moses settled into his new life as a shepherd for his father-in-law for forty years. Every day for forty years Moses lived and worked in the wilderness. Every day for forty years Moses herded sheep—in the wilderness.

I ask my fifth graders why they think it is significant that Moses spent time in the wilderness. We talk about how many of God's great men spent time there: Abraham, David, Elijah, Paul, and even Jesus. Before God put His chosen men

God's people need to learn to follow Him before He will allow them to lead others.

93

to work, He frequently placed them in the wilderness. God's people need to learn to follow Him before He will allow them to lead others. In the wilderness there is no one but God to depend on. Moses would spend virtually the rest of his life in the wilderness. He needed to know what that meant.

Then I ask my fifth graders why Moses would need to know about herding sheep. They get it that the recalcitrant group Moses is going to end up shepherding through the wilds would make any herd of sheep look like a well-trained drill team!

A STEP IN THE RIGHT DIRECTION

Meanwhile, back in Egypt, another movement was going on. After four hundred years of captivity, God's people put in a call for His help. Had they been calling for some time and He was waiting for the prophesied four hundred years to pass, or did it take them four hundred years to finally get around to calling? I suspect the latter.

I recognize the lack of urgency in my prayer life until I find myself or someone I love in deep need. When things are going well, we think this world a friendly place where we can live in peace and prosperity without needing to disturb God. It's only when we realize that this world is hard and cruel and godless that we know we should never be comfortable here.

When things are going well, we think this world a friendly place where we can live in peace and prosperity without needing to disturb God.

For many years God's people had lived the good life in Egypt, and they seemed content there. But just as we are not destined for the "good life" found in this world, the Israelites were not destined for life in Egypt. They had forgotten who they were: children of Abraham, Isaac, and Jacob, and recipients of the covenant promise. They had forgotten whose they were: God's chosen people. The Lord wanted them to remember what He had promised them through their forefathers: a land of their own, a great nation, a blessing to all nations through them. These Israelites had a noble purpose for existing, a *holy* purpose, and it was not to live quietly in someone else's land under the dominion of someone else's gods.

It took turmoil and torment to get God's people to remember to call on Him, but they finally called. And when they called, He was ready with the answer: Moses. Before God's people ever called, a baby had been born and saved from death. A young man had been raised knowing all about Egypt and also about his own heritage. A shepherd had learned to survive in the wilderness and lead a flock through the desert—eighty years to train the right man for the job. Everything was ready for God's people when they decided to call on Him. Now all that remained was for God to call on Moses.

GOD MOVES IN ON MOSES

One day, God made an extraordinary visit to an ordinary place called Mount Horeb (or Mount Sinai). While Moses tended his father-in-law's sheep on the mountain, he saw something most spectacular: a bush that burned but did not burn up. He went to investigate the phenomenon and became involved in something even more phenomenal. As he approached the bush, God spoke from it and called his name. Moses answered the call and also the command to remove his shoes. He stood on holy ground. Out of reverence for God and acknowledgment of his unworthiness to be in His presence, Moses removed his shoes and hid his face.

When the theory that God most likely exists becomes the certainty that He is, one has no choice but to bow.

Can you imagine the awe, even the fear, in that encounter? When God steps into the life of one of His children, when He becomes "real" for the first time, when the theory that God most likely exists becomes the certainty that He *is*, one has no choice but to bow. There is no way to stand before the awesome presence of the Almighty.

God introduced Himself to Moses as the God of his fathers Abraham, Isaac, and Jacob, and He informed Moses that He had heard His people's cry for help, He was concerned about their suffering, He had come down to rescue His people from Egypt, and He would lead them out of Egypt to the land He had promised them on oath. God told Moses that *He* would do it. I'm sure Moses rejoiced in that good news . . . until God's next newsflash: I want you to go tell Pharaoh that I am going to do this!

You know how some things sound really good in theory, but the reality is something entirely different? Imagine how Moses felt when he heard how God was going to get His people out of Egypt. He was going to use Moses. Remembering the last time he had been in Egypt, Moses rightfully assumed that he would not be welcomed by either the Egyptians or the Israelites. The shepherd surely wondered if he was the ideal person for this job.

Moses' first question to God reflected his uncertainty: "Who am I?" God assured Moses it didn't matter who he was, because He would be with him. So Moses' next question was, "Who are You?" Specifically he asked, "Suppose I go to the Israelites and say to them, 'The God of your fathers has sent me to you,' and they ask me, 'What is his name?' Then what shall I tell them?" Moses knew he would enter a land of many Egyptian gods and an environment where God's own people had not called on His name in many years. Which God should Moses say was sending him? How should the Israelites address the God who was coming to call on them? Moses needed to know for the people and for himself.

So God introduced Himself. The answer was powerful in its simplicity: "I AM WHO I AM." Does that make sense? He is what *is*. The God who called on Moses to call on His children is *the* God, the author of all that exists, all that *is*.

Furthermore, the Almighty was about to become very *present* with His people. He told Moses to tell them, "I AM has sent me to you. . . . The LORD, the God of your fathers—the God of Abraham, Isaac, and Jacob—has sent me to you." *That God,* the One they'd heard of their whole lives—He *exists*. And He knows what's going on with His children. The same God who remembered their fathers had not forgotten them. Not only did that great God know their fathers, He wanted to know them. He wanted the relationship to continue. He said, "This is my name *forever,* the name by which I am to be *remembered* from generation to generation." God gave Moses His personal name, the name by which He wanted to be known, and He allowed Moses, even encouraged Moses, to tell His name to His children. I AM. Jehovah. Yahweh. The LORD. The Creator of the universe was seeking a relationship with His children, and He wanted them to know Him personally. He wanted them to remember Him forever.

Even with all God told Moses about Himself, it took some persuading to get Moses to go back to Egypt. When he feared the people wouldn't believe him, God gave Moses a miraculous sign to prove he was from God. When he worried that he was not eloquent enough to make God's speeches, God told Moses that He had made his mouth and could certainly help him use it. When he couldn't think of any other plausible excuses, Moses eventually just begged God to send someone else. ("Here am I. Send someone else.") And although God was not happy with Moses' reluctance, He did tell him that his brother Aaron had already been sent to meet him on the way and to act as his assistant. Finally, with the staff of God's guaranteed presence clutched tightly in his hand, Moses packed up his life again and headed back to Egypt.

GOD MOVES IN ON EGYPT

When Moses and Aaron first told the Israelites that God had heard their cries and was concerned with their misery, the people bowed in humility and worshiped in gratitude. But they had a little trouble maintaining that posture. Pharaoh rejected the first invitation to let God's people go into the desert to worship, and he not only refused to acknowledge the Lord's right to ask but made the Israelites' lives worse to prove he didn't care about their God. When their lives got harder, God's people began to question not only God's leaders but also God's leadership. This will become a familiar pattern. *Watch out when you're watching God's children of Israel because you're seeing the nature that guides all God's children.* When God unleashed His power upon the land of Egypt, whom do you think He wanted most to convince of His might? Was it for the eyes of Pharaoh or Israel that the Almighty declared His sovereignty and let justice roll?

While Pharaoh was thinking he was powerful and Israel was wondering if the Lord was strong enough, the Sovereign King of the universe demonstrated who was "large and in charge" in the land, and God vs. Egypt was no contest. God will win *any* battle He is in. Those who choose His side will also win. Pharaoh thought he could stand against God and refused to let God's people go, so God demanded them back.

But God's final plague would not only inflict death upon the people of Egypt; it would give a picture of life to His own people. Sovereign God had given His enemies what they deserved; that's what justice is. He was also going to teach His own how they would be able to escape justice. God was going to show His children His redemption. He would begin to teach them about the saving power of blood. He would give them a glimpse of the horizontal and vertical surfaces that would be covered in that blood. He would tell His people about the perfect lamb that would be necessary as a sacrifice, the innocent one who would die as a substitute for the one who deserved to die. He would

> *God will win any battle He is in. Those who choose His side will also win.*

introduce His people to bread that is life. And He would convince them of the need for obedience and the need for faith in the God who calls them to obey.

It would be a night no one would ever forget. In fact, God's people would be commanded *not* to forget. They were ordered not only to remember but also to tell everyone about it. Remember so you can remind! God told them what kind of lamb to use, when to sacrifice it, what to do with its blood, how to cook the lamb, how to eat it, and what to eat with it. They were also told to eat with their traveling clothes on, with shoes on their feet, and with staff in hand. And they were to eat in haste. Eat hurrying up, standing up, packed up, dressed up, and ready to pull out, because when the night is over, you're all out of here!

Remember so you can remind!

And it came to pass just as the Lord had said. Death came in the night. So did deliverance from death. Passover: what a concept! What a gift! The dispenser of life and death passed over all of Egypt, and in any household without the covering of blood (including the household of Pharaoh himself), people died. But God's people lived, and the next day they were given much of Egypt's riches and were urged out of the country by the very man who had previously refused to let them leave. Before God sent Moses into Egypt, He had told him it would happen just as it did; not only would Pharaoh let God's people go, he would drive them out, and they would leave with the plunder of Egypt in their pockets. And so they did. After four hundred years of being settled in a foreign land, God's pilgrim people were on the road again, heading for their own land, guided by a bright promise and a powerful God.

GOD MOVES 'EM OUT OF EGYPT

Few scenes in world history would compete with the Exodus for sheer spectacle and evidence of God's hand. The numbers alone were astounding. Seventy people had entered Egypt 430 years before, and two to three million people would leave. They exited with flocks and herds, wagons and baggage, the bones of Joseph, and the riches of Egypt. What a sight it must have been as literally millions of people and animals walked out of Egypt and headed to the Promised Land.

Behold the phenomenon as God Himself headed up the convoy! With a pillar of cloud in the day and a pillar of fire at night, God visibly led His people where He wanted them to go. They had all the evidence they needed to believe that God could do what He said He would. He had thoroughly whipped the most powerful nation on earth in order to free His people from the ruthless bondage of slavery, and He placed a sign of His presence and leadership in front of their eyes every day. A miraculous delivery was followed by miraculous guidance. Theirs was an *Almighty* God. His might was *visible*. They had seen His power with their own eyes! He was a God in whom they could have utter confidence, right? We would think so if we weren't painfully aware of our weak and fearful nature when faced with a threat. Really, let's be fair about this. What were they supposed to think when they suddenly found themselves between the devil and the deep Red Sea?

It seems that Pharaoh had had a change of heart or a change of mind or a serious attack of overreaching pride. Weren't ten encounters with the God of Israel enough? Pharaoh didn't think so, because he decided to go into the desert to retrieve his slaves. You might wonder how he found the horses to pull more than six hundred chariots since his livestock had been wiped out by plague. I'm thinking God saved the horses so He could once again save His people. Before Pharaoh even began his pursuit of the Israelites into the desert, God told Moses that Pharaoh would come after them and that He would be waiting when Pharaoh came. The Lord said He would gain glory for Himself through Pharaoh and his army, and the Egyptians would know that He was "I am." And as before, I think God also had in mind some other people who needed to know.

When God's people looked up and saw Pharaoh's army charging after them, they quickly forgot about the God who had so recently and miraculously delivered them, and they thought only of the Egyptian army behind them and the Red Sea before them. They lost sight of the God who was sitting in a cloud right over their heads. Or maybe they thought, *But this is different. How can He save us from this?*

We have the same kind of belief in God. Sure, we believe, God did *that*, but what about *this*? Remember Jesus and Martha at the grave of Lazarus? Martha had seen things and heard things, and she knew Jesus could heal. But Jesus wanted her to know more of Him: He wanted her to believe that He was also Lord over death. And when Jesus convinced her that He could raise Lazarus from death, she then couldn't be entirely sure He was also Lord over decay. When Jesus ordered the stone rolled away from the tomb, Martha cried out, "But, Lord! It's been four days!" That's the way we humans are. We're ruled by a "but, Lord!" kind of belief. We're not sure how far we can extend our faith in who God is and what God really wants to do for us. So we shouldn't judge the Israelites too harshly as they saw the wrath of hell rushing down on them and began to wonder what they'd signed up for in following God into the wilderness.

We shouldn't judge, but really! (Okay, so it's hard not to judge *others'* lack of faith. . . .) Think about what they had just witnessed! They had seen miraculous deliverance. They daily saw God leading them. How could they lose sight so soon?

Because their eyes were on the chariots at their heels rather than the pillar of God at their heads.

9 REMEMBERING IS MADE OF THIS

DESERT DWELLING

Only be careful, and watch yourselves closely
so that you do not forget the things your eyes have seen
or let them slip from your heart as long as you live.
Teach them to your children and to their children after them.

—DEUTERONOMY 4:9

EXODUS 14:13–40:38; LEVITICUS

My maternal grandmother lived to be a hundred years old, testifying, I'm afraid, to the old adage that "Ugly things don't break." That sounds really mean, and to be fair she did sort of mellow a bit after the age of ninety-five or so when she got deaf and wasn't sure she understood enough of her surroundings to complain about them. Grannie was a tiny little thing, but she had an intimidating presence. And not just to her children and grandchildren and her ornery but sweet little mate, who finally passed away to find some peace, but also to others, like the elderly gentleman who made the mistake of sitting in her designated chair in the retirement-home breakfast room and received a swift whack to the head with a rolled-up newspaper!

Our family celebrated Grannie's "last birthday—again" with the largest celebrations taking place on her ninetieth and ninety-fifth birthdays. On those two occasions, complete with cake and all hands on deck to celebrate, the family "remembered" the highlights of her life with amusing narrative, original songs, and a fine decade-by-decade historical perspective of the times in which she had lived. She may have been tiny, and she was frequently disagreeable, but our family matriarch was a formidable female and a very accomplished individual, especially for a woman of her time, and we all enjoyed hearing about her. In remembering Grannie Jackson's life, we gained some perspective on our own. The precious memories that a family holds is usually what holds a family together . . . the Jackson family and the family of God.

At this point in the historical narrative of God's people—when the Israelites are about to cross the Red Sea—I tell my fifth graders there is a word I want them to remember for the rest of the year as we study about God. In fact, it's a word I want them to remember for the rest of their lives. It's a word that even God considers vital for us to remember. The word is *remember!* It is absolutely essential that we remember something important, even crucial, if we are to succeed on any journey with God. We must *remember God,* the God whose infallible character we believe in, whose loving care we have witnessed, whose might we can trust, who knows where He wants us to go.

God wanted Israel to remember what they had seen and were seeing. He wanted them to remember His power over Egypt and over the very forces of nature. He wanted them to remember that He had chosen them, He loved them, and He had saved them by their faith in the blood of the lamb. He wanted them to remember that He had delivered them from the bonds of slavery and He was still their very visible guide to freedom. Many times in His future dealings with His children, the admonition would ring out from the voice of God: "Remember!" "Don't forget!" So to help them remember, God gave His people something really memorable!

Moses didn't know how God would deliver; he just knew God would deliver. That's faith.

At this early point in their journey and many times in the days to come, the children of Israel would be well served by a leader who did remember God. Moses, remembering the God He met in a burning bush, remembering the God who had empowered him to stand up to Pharaoh, remembering the God who had decimated Pharaoh's realm, believed that God could and would deliver him yet again. He cried out to the people as they stood in terror before the swirling waters of the Red Sea, "Do not be afraid. Stand firm and you will see the deliverance the LORD will bring you today. . . . The LORD will fight for you; you need only to be still." Note that Moses didn't know *how* God would deliver; he just knew God *would* deliver. That's faith. And as for God, man, did He deliver!

GRAND OPENING

The parting of the Red Sea may be the singular most impressive miracle God has ever done, and there are some really impressive ones in His arsenal of miracles! When God's prophets and leaders wanted to remind the people of His goodness toward them, they nearly always mentioned the Red Sea. We've seen the movies, but to see this in real life in real time must have been awesome, literally. (I tell my kids that awe is like the physiology that produces the sound of the word. It is a jaw-dropping experience. When you say the word, your mouth hangs open. Likewise when you experience the sensation!)

The angel of the Lord, who traveled with the cloud before the people, and the cloud itself moved behind the people and stood between Israel and Pharaoh's army. It became dark on Pharaoh's side and light on Israel's side. Then Moses, at God's command, stretched out his staff—the staff that represented the presence and power of God—over the sea. The sea began to divide. (By the way, it's impossible to "divide" water. Oops, I guess that's what a miracle is! It's something impossible!) And God opened the sea. He drove it back with a strong east wind (the breath of angels?), and the Israelites walked across on dry land with a wall of water on either side.

Movies depict a dramatic scene as the people walk between the walls of water. I especially love the scene in *The Prince of Egypt* as the fish are visible, and the people stumble along with terrified expressions on their faces. I imagine it was a frightening sight, but I'm just as sure that the movies are totally inadequate, because their special effects are nothing compared to God's. Consider the logistics of the Israelites crossing the Red Sea in one night. If three and a half million people walked two abreast, I have read that it would have taken thirty-five days and nights for them to cross, so as many as five thousand would have needed to cross at a time to make it in a night. The sea would have probably been opened three miles wide to accomplish that. It's hard to wrap my human mind around the dimensions of the miracle God did that night. However He did it, God performed in such a way that it would awe His followers and petrify His adversaries for decades to come. And he wasn't finished.

Not only would God take care of the Red Sea; He would take care of Pharaoh's army. After the Israelites got across the dry seabed, the angel-cloud barricade lifted, and Israel's Pharaoh-following foes tried to cross after them. The Almighty looked down from the pillar of fire and cloud and threw their army into disarray by causing the chariot wheels to come off and slow them down. When that happened, the Egyptians began saying something that many opponents in the future would recognize as true: "No fair! The Lord is fighting for them against us!" To prove their point, the Lord ordered Moses to stretch out his staff across the seabed once more, and the waters that had been held in place by God closed over the army of Pharaoh and wiped them out. What a night! "And when the Israelites saw the great power the LORD displayed against the Egyptians, the people feared the LORD and put their trust in him and in Moses his servant."

That is, until they got thirsty . . . or hungry . . . or tired . . . or . . .

BREADTH OF BOUNTY

Right after they left the Red Sea, Moses led the people into the desert, and for three days they couldn't find water. The people began to complain. It was only the beginning of the litany of woes they would present to Moses and God before this trip would end. They were dying of thirst. The water was bitter. They were going to starve. Okay, there was bread, but it was boring having bread every day; they wanted meat. I'm surprised Moses didn't level a few whacks with his staff upon the people instead of upon the rock to produce water.

I'm overwhelmed at the graciousness of God continuing to give them sustenance when they were so ungrateful. Hmm. Did I just step on my own toes? How hard it is to continue in faith that God will deliver daily! How tempting it is to gather too much and risk having it all ruined, or not to gather at all out of laziness or lack of foresight! How human it is to want "different" or "more exciting" or simply variety, which is, after all, the spice of life! Truly, how different are we regarding the Lord's bounty? The Israelites in the wilderness irritate me to no end, but what sobers me is that I fear I would have been just like them: complaining and questioning every decision, wondering if the leader was really being led by God, wondering if God was sure this was the best way to do it, just in general wondering instead of trusting. Since I last taught this lesson to fifth graders, I have been to Israel and through the

Jordanian desert. I may be a little kinder the next time I teach it. That is one bleak landscape, and even traveling by bus and having bottles of water wasn't enough to keep me from getting irritable!

There was a lot of humanity to reckon with as God led His people toward His promise. First of all, there were simply a lot of humans. The scope of what God did on a daily basis is staggering. According to an army quartermaster general, Moses would have to provide 1,500 tons of food each day; 4,000 tons of firewood to cook it; and 11,000,000 gallons of water for consumption and utility use. If it had been transported by train cars, they would have stretched over 1,800 miles. That's every day. For forty years. Every time they camped (which was every time the cloud stopped and stood in one place at God's command), it would have required as much as 750 square miles, or a space two-thirds the size of Rhode Island. The logistics are almost beyond comprehension.

How hard it is to continue in faith that God will deliver daily!

And, adding to the amplitude of humanity, those humans were awfully human. Every day God led His ungrateful, whining, cantankerous chosen people across the desert toward the Promised Land. And every day He probably had to remind Himself why He had chosen them.

For three months the Israelites traveled toward Mount Sinai. On the way they benefited from God's continual care as daily and miraculously He filled their empty bellies and quenched their parched throats, and He did it all in the face of galloping ingratitude. He also introduced them to another part of His program for them: not only would God provide; He would protect. Soon after leaving Egypt, God needed to deliver His children from still another set of cousins: the Amalekites, fierce and war-loving descendants of Esau. God delivered with the leadership of Joshua and the upheld hands of Moses (who got by with a little help from his friends). And after the victory, God insisted Moses write down His promise for posterity: at some time in the future God would complete the victory over the people who had attacked His children without provocation. His specific words were, "I will completely blot out the memory of Amalek from under heaven." Yikes! And we're going to see Him do it later on. We could probably witness His victories for His children today if we only had the eyes to see.

Next, with *provision* and *protection* thoroughly demonstrated, God led His people toward *promotion*. They had been the children of God for a long time, with all the attributes that implies. It was time for God's children to do a little growing up. It was time for them to go to school.

HIGH STATUTES

God prepared to take the next step, a very large one, toward molding a nation out of three million grumbling, demanding, and ungrateful individuals. He was going to form an undisciplined mob into His chosen people. They were children unaccustomed to following rules. They had been the offspring of patriarchs who acted on visions, dreams, and signs. They had been slaves at the whim of capricious masters. But they had little experience governing themselves or being governed by God Himself. That was going to change. The time had come when God wanted everyone to know what He wanted. It was time for them to find out what it meant to be the people of God.

Moses' first meeting with God had been on Mount Sinai. Now God called out to Moses from the mountain a second time and invited him to another face-to-face visit. Exodus 19 tells the story of God calling on Moses once again to take a message to His people. Tell them, God said, "You yourselves have seen what I did to Egypt, and how I carried you on eagles' wings and brought you to myself. Now if you obey me fully and keep my covenant, then out of all nations you will be my treasured possession. Although the whole earth is mine, you will be for me a kingdom of priests and a holy nation." God told them they had witnessed what He does for His people. He is a keeper of covenant. Were they? God had chosen them to reveal Him to the rest of the world. They were His representatives to people who could know Him no other way. They were the instruments through which He would save the entire world. And there were a few expectations for how the people of God would demonstrate that they are the people of God. What would be their response? When they heard God's words, delivered through Moses, the people vowed to "do everything the LORD has said." They probably meant it at the time.

At the Lord's command the people cleansed themselves and were consecrated. They got ready physically and spiritually, set themselves apart from routine in order to meet God in worship, and with the warning of God ringing in their ears not to approach the mountain, God's people waited for His arrival—a phenomenon of sight and sound! A thick cloud came down on the mountain. Thunder boomed, lightning blazed, and smoke billowed. The whole mountain trembled violently. Then from the trembling, booming, billowing mountain came the sound of a trumpet blaring. And this was not Israel's marching band sounding the trumpets. It had to be the trumpets of angels as the sound from the mountain grew louder and louder. I bet the mountain wasn't the only thing trembling that day as God came down from heaven to Mount Sinai and called Moses up to meet Him there.

God's voice rang out from the mountain. And God's own finger engraved upon the tablets of stone His holy commandments for His people. The One who spoke the words that created life began to speak the words that would teach man how God wanted him to live his life. God's covenant with Abraham and his descendants had been a one-way covenant, a covenant of promise from God. In His words to Abraham, God expressed what He would do because of who He was. The covenant given on Mount Sinai was going to be a two-way deal. What parameters of behavior would be expected from these covenant people who would represent God in the world? They are to live in worship and in relationship, to love and revere their God, and to love and regard their fellowman.

Laws Regarding the High and Holy

God, *the* God, demands preeminence in the hearts of those who would follow Him. He must be worshiped. There must be nothing above Him: no one, no thing, no pursuit. Nothing can be substituted in His place. He made all things, and nothing created can supplant the One who created it. How incredibly presumptuous it is for the created to attempt creation, to try to make a god that can be controlled by human hands or minds. A god one can make is not a god worth worshiping. God alone is Creator, and God alone is worthy of worship.

His name, the name that represents who He is, is holy and is meant to be used for good. The name of God is never to be misused in word or deed, never for evil or selfish reasons, never for empty or mundane pursuits that would benefit only the user. Since God's name tells of His presence ("I am"), then He should be considered present when His name is used.

God is holy. He must be honored and regarded as holy. He even wants regular and dedicated time within His people's lives when their whirl of daily living is put aside and Holy God is remembered and revered. The relationship with God is to be primary in the lives of His children.

LAWS REGARDING THE WEAK AND LOWLY

The first four of the Ten Commandments clearly state that God matters above all things. Those four are difficult enough to keep, even knowing that God is worthy of obedience. Still, if honoring God was all that was required, we might be able to pull it off. Unfortunately, four out of ten commandments still leaves six commandments that make law keeping onerous to those of us who don't consider other people quite as worthy of honor as God is. As someone once said:

> To live above with the One I love, oh, that will be glory!
> But to live below with those I know, well, that's another story!

Wouldn't life be far easier and more pleasant if there weren't so many *others* to get in the way of godly living? God is easy to honor and to love. But it gets really difficult when He tells us that one of the most visible ways we honor and love Him is by honoring and loving His other children, even those who aren't very honorable or lovable. If only other people didn't matter so much to God, it might not matter so much how we treated them. However, they do matter very much to Him, and He cares very much how much they matter to us as well.

The six commandments that deal with how God wants His people to act toward others sound pretty cut-and-dried and even, dare I say, doable when one just reads through them. It's understandable how the Israelites and their descendants, the Jews of the New Testament who still believed in the rule of the old Law, could feel a bit self-congratulatory when they viewed the checklist look of the last six commandments. If they didn't commit murder, adultery, or grand theft, and didn't lie under oath, they looked pretty good. A couple of the six were harder to pin down, such as the essence of honoring and not coveting, but most were pretty concrete about what one was not supposed to do.

If we look at the letter of the law and never at the heart of the law, it is always going to be easier to keep the law.

I grew up in a time and in a church where Christianity was defined and recognized by what we didn't do. If the checklist of don'ts was satisfactorily completed, we were acceptable. It was easier, but I'm not too sure it was what was intended, even in the beginning of the law. If we look at the letter of the law and never at the heart of the law, it is always going to be easier to keep the law. But God has this thing about heart. He frequently seems more interested in *why* we do what we do than in *what* we do.

The chapters that follow the giving of the Ten Commandments in Exodus 20 expand on those ten "summary" rules for moral living. God doesn't necessarily mention the heart, but He makes it clear that He will not sanction a life lived only for self with no regard for others. We let ourselves off lightly if we think we have fulfilled the whole Law by adhering to the letter of God's Law and never looking beyond the simple "thou shalt nots" to what lay in the heart of God.

As a summary for good behavior, we can't beat the Ten Commandments, the epitome of moral law upon which all religious, family, civil, and criminal law is built. God could have stopped right there and let man, as he has done, look for the loopholes and exceptions and prioritize things as he saw fit. But the One who created man knows a little about man's priorities and tendencies to seek exceptions. So in the chapters and books that follow the giving of the Ten Commandments, God got specific about how He wanted His people to behave. He got specific to the tune of 613 laws given to Israel. (I didn't personally count them, but someone who likes to do that sort of thing did, and I took his word for it.)

Exodus and Leviticus provide specific, detailed statutes for every feast and holy day: laws for the Sabbath, sacrifices, priests and Levites, worship, and regulations for building the tabernacle. These sections both include and foreshadow the true worship from the heart that God will require in His new covenant, and they speak boldly of blood, sacrifice, and substitution being the requirements for atonement, recompense, and reconciliation. There are also precise precepts for family living: laws for marriage, rules for inheritance, regulations for the discipline of children (which I enjoy sharing with my fifth graders since they involve a lot of stoning). The most interesting sections of the Law to read are the civil and criminal sections in Exodus 21–22 and Deuteronomy 22–25 as God anticipated mankind's foibles and told him how to prepare for them or repair them. Not a single aspect of mankind's life was neglected in the giving of the Law. The apostle Paul called the Law a "schoolmaster," and great care was certainly taken to teach man how to relate to God and to his fellowman. The Law given on Mount Sinai teaches us a lot about God and a lot about the kind of people God wants as His representatives. The Law revealed God's values, the Law defined sin, and the Law described what holy living looks like.

God indeed gave a lot of rules to His chosen people. They had been set apart by Him to live set-apart lives. They were designed to call attention to their holy God and His holy purpose by their holy living. It would be wholly hard for them to do.

SHORT-TERM MEMORY

In fact, God's people couldn't even keep up godly living while their leader was on Sinai getting the Law. While Moses and God were still on the mountain, the people went to Aaron and begged him to make them new (read that as *better*) gods in place of the One who had brought them into the desert and seemed to have swallowed up "this fellow Moses" on the smoking mountain.

Okay, I'm going to give them an excuse here, because I suspect I would have needed one had I been there. Just a couple of months before Mount Sinai, these people had been snatched out of what was a sure thing, even if it was surely bad. In Egypt they had at least known what to expect, and there is security in just knowing. The God who had introduced Himself to them quite recently and was now leading them quite visibly was admittedly powerful and undoubtedly fierce with those who stood against Him. In fact, He was a bit frightening. And to most of them, Moses was likely only a rumor. With no big screen to project him to the masses, most of the people had probably never laid eyes on Moses. He would eventually assume almost mythical proportions, but at this point both Moses and his God were somewhat mysterious and incomprehensible. Really, what would you have thought under the circumstances? Something big was happening on that mountain, but it was hard to tell what it was, and it was just as hard to trust someone they didn't really quite get yet. I'm prone to excuse the Israelites' comportment, because I recognize in their behavior my own. The Lord, however, took their conduct more personally.

God was, you might say, mightily displeased at their display of faithlessness. He told Moses to go down from the mountain, because "your people" (not God's!) were busy worshiping their new handmade god. How quickly they had turned away from Him. Before Moses headed up the mountain, the people had sworn allegiance to the Lord, but by the time Moses headed back down the mountain, they had chosen another lord. God's anger burned, and He wanted to destroy the faithless people and build a nation out of Moses. He certainly could have done it, but Moses beseeched the Lord not to give ammunition to His enemies by destroying His own people so soon after delivering them. Moses reminded Him of His promise to Abraham, and God "remembered" and relented. Each of God's responses indicates His nature: in justice He could have legitimately destroyed the people for rebelling against Him, but instead He chose mercy and another chance for His people to obey.

With God's grace in his heart and God's Law in his hands, Moses headed down the mountain to the people. On the way back to camp, Joshua, who had accompanied Moses part of the way, heard "the sound of war" in the camp. Moses told him it wasn't the sound of war. It was *worse* than that: it was singing! The people were rejoicing in their blatant disobedience as they danced around their new golden god.

After getting God to relent in His anger, Moses released his own anger when he saw the dancing, singing, reveling of rampant rebellion. He smashed the tablets, crushed the idol, and drew a line in the sand. Like an early version of Colonel Travis at the Alamo, Moses told the true believers to step toward him and make a commitment. The Levites rallied with Moses and at his command killed about three thousand rebellious revelers. Then Moses turned back toward God, whose heart he trusted, and interceded for the people he couldn't trust.

Moses' next trip up the mountain led to a renewal of the Law by God, a renewal of covenant by the people, and an enlightening experience for everyone. While earlier in His presence, Moses had begged for God's continued and manifest presence in leading the Israelites, and when God agreed, Moses asked for a little proof. He said, "Show me your glory." God told him that no one could see His face and

Seeing God's back means we can only see where He has passed by.

live but that He would cause His "goodness" to pass in front of Moses. What a picture of God's magnificence as we read how He placed Moses in the cleft of a rock and covered Moses with His hand as He passed by. Moses' brief glimpse of just the "back" of God caused his face to glow so radiantly that he had to veil himself before the people could even look at him. I have read that seeing God's back means we can only see where He has passed by. In other words, we know who He is by what He has done and how He acts. Moses would certainly witness the goodness of God in the years to come as He would continue to deal faithfully and lovingly with His people who offered little faithfulness and a dearth of love.

LONG-TERM RELATIONSHIP

The Israelites camped at Mount Sinai for about a year. While there, they began to get organized religiously and governmentally. Priests were called out from the tribe of Levi, and all the rituals of worship were established. Moses, with his father-in-law's encouragement and God's backing, established the civil proceedings for governing the people. And the people built a house for God.

The God who delivered by His power would now direct by His presence.

With the precise plans given by God Himself, the Israelites constructed the tabernacle, which represented the presence of God and the pattern of salvation. God's house would be the center of Israelite travels and Israelite life. When they marched, the tabernacle would be in the center of the processional. When they camped, the tabernacle would be in the center of the camp. God called His people to make worship central to their very existence. The book of Exodus, which began with the oppression of God's chosen people, closes with the planning, building, and, in the final verses, the filling of the tabernacle as God's glory came to dwell in the presence of His people. God is *with* His people. The God who delivered by His power would now direct by His presence.

10 ROAD TRIP

WILDERNESS WANDERINGS

They refused to listen and failed to remember the miracles
you performed among them. . . . But you are a forgiving God,
gracious and compassionate, slow to anger and abounding in love.
Therefore you did not desert them.

—NEHEMIAH 9:17

NUMBERS–DEUTERONOMY

Preparing children to go on a long road trip is exacting to say the least. After the planning is done, there's laundry and packing to do, and there's persuading the children that the destination is going to be worth all the preliminaries. When the family finally gets on the trail, the rules of the road are laid down, the benefits are laid out, the promise is laid forth, and a rewarding outcome is anticipated by everyone. While the preparation is only exhausting, the trip itself frequently borders on excruciating. I have spent many a long car trip with my rear end near the roof of the car and my face and hands in the backseat dealing with one "event" or another. I repeatedly begged to drive, but my husband always persuaded me that it was man's work and should really be done by a real man. My job was entertainment and containment, provision and submission, and, when necessary, appropriate violence. Bickering and whining, selfishness and willfulness, and general ingratitude for the benefits being bestowed were to be dealt with severely before wholesale revolt could break out. Traveling with two children was grueling. Multiply that by a million, and it still doesn't get close to the "joys" Moses experienced as the children of Israel hit the road toward the Promised Land.

In the opening chapters of Numbers, God instructed Moses to conduct a census of the people, who were then camped at the base of Mount Sinai, and get them ready to travel. They were to be purified, packed up, and placed in their marching order. By all rights, it should have been a grateful group headed for glorious gain. They had just spent a year in proximity to the God of promise. He now occupied the house they had built for Him, and He had explained how they should live with Him and among their fellow men. His Law had been laid down, and now it was time to go and claim their inheritance.

A TRAVELOGUE OF TRAVAIL

If anything points out how law cannot save us or even change us, it is the sights and sounds of the Israelites journeying toward the Promised Land. Just three days out from Mount Sinai, they complained about the hardships they were enduring. Before Sinai, God had somewhat tolerated the people's complaints, but things seemed a bit different after He told them what He wanted from them. This time their tirade resulted in a visible reminder that the God who demands honor and worship is a God who doesn't appreciate His worshipers grumbling against Him. The divine Judge's judgment on the whining was swift and visible. I'm guessing He aimed a few lightning bolts in the campers' direction, because the Scripture says that flames consumed the outskirts of the camp. Let the learning begin!

Unfortunately, they didn't appear to be astute students. Within a short time the people were complaining again, this time about God's provision. The miracle bread that greeted them every morning was soon considered inadequate, and they began to crave "more" and "different" and "better." (Anything sound familiar?) They wailed for the good life in Egypt, where good things were all around them. I wonder if God gritted His teeth when they yearned for what they defined as "good" in that heathen country. What a slap in the face of God, not only to criticize and reject what He freely gave, but to long for the days when they were surrounded by empty, pagan gods.

After turning up their noses at God's bread, the people demanded meat. So God gave them meat. In fact, the Giver gave them so much meat, in the form of quails that flew into the camp, that He told Moses the people would have it coming out of their nostrils until they loathed meat.

Moses wanted to know, "Would they have enough if flocks and herds were slaughtered for them? Would they have enough if all the fish in the sea were caught for them?" Moses was sick and tired of the people's complaints and began to wonder if God could provide enough to shut them up. I look at that question Moses asked God, and I wonder if God heard it this way: "Will *anything* ever be *enough* for these people?" Even my fifth graders recognize that the answer to that question is no. And let it stand as an admonition to all of us: there is never enough for the ungrateful person. Every day of their lives in the wilderness, Israel was privileged to see God at work for them. Not only had they witnessed the miracles God had performed in redeeming and delivering them from bondage, but they also daily observed God's presence, provision, and protection. There was never a day when God's cloud disappeared from their sight. They never awoke to a single morning without manna on the ground or in their Sabbath preparation bag. Every day God led. Every day God fed. But it was never enough.

There is never enough for the ungrateful person.

THANKS, BUT NO THANKS

In spite of Israel's conspicuous ingratitude and their concerted disobedience, God continued with His plan. (Bask in the knowledge that He continually does that—with those ungrateful people who lived way back then and with the ungrateful people who live among us and who, in fact, are us.) Israel's God led them right up to the door of Canaan and prepared to deliver on His promise. It was finally time for them to take what He offered.

The Lord instructed Moses to send twelve men, one from each tribe, to explore the land He was going to *give* them. Don't for a moment lose sight of the promise that this land was to be a gift from God. Moses told the twelve to bring back a thorough scouting report. He even told them to do their best to bring back some fruit to show the waiting people. And then the Bible has a little parenthetical notation that reads, "It was the season for the first ripe grapes." Any child who has been in Bible class can tell you the significance of that sentence. The twelve "spies" spent forty days checking out the land that God promised would *flow* (a further promise of the Lord's extravagant generosity) with milk and honey. On my recent trip to Israel, our Israeli guide explained that the phrase means the bounty provided by the huge flocks of milk-giving goats in the hills and the sweet profusion of honey-producing date palms in the valleys—all of which sounds much more prosaic but eminently more practical than any vision we might have entertained of sticky fluids bubbling up from the ground!

When the explorers came back, they carried proof that indeed their future home was as God had represented. The Lord was giving them a fertile and flourishing land.

When faith is absent, there is always a but.

The men returned with figs and pomegranates and a single cluster of grapes (not a single grape as one of my on-the-path-but-fuzzy-with-the-details students volunteered), a cluster so large two men had to carry it on a pole between them. (That would have been some grape!) The fruit they brought back was a spectacular representation of the abundance God was presenting to them. The twelve men proclaimed that the land was as rich and beautiful as God had promised, but . . .

When faith is absent, there is always a *but.*

The good news was that it was a great land. The bad news was that inside the great land great big people inhabited great big, fortified cities. Consequently, ten of the twelve men declared there was no way the land could be taken. Caleb, one of two of the twelve, said, "We *should* go up and take possession . . . for we *can* certainly do it." But the ten detractors argued, "We can't . . . they are stronger than we are." They were absolutely correct in recognizing that *they* couldn't, that *they* were weak. But God had told them He was *giving* them this land. This was the same God who had gone in and taken them from the most powerful nation on earth and then had declared Himself on their side for all time in all situations.

I don't think I've ever seen a worse case of short-term memory loss than in these people. They vex me to no end, but what scares me is that I keep seeing myself in them. God has told me in every way He can that the battle has already been won and that all I have to do is sign on with Him and line up with Him, and I will be on the winning side. Still, those big, bad fortresses filled with big, bad people in this big, bad world can take my eyes off the power of God.

When Caleb argued that the land *could* be possessed, the dissidents stirred the entire congregation against him. You know, it is one thing to question whether God *will* do something; it is entirely different to question whether He *can* do it. But all the people could see was the strength of the enemy and their own weakness. So the community grumbled (surprise!) against Moses and wailed (again!) to return to Egypt. In fact, the group stirred up each other all night and decided that in the morning they would choose a new leader and return to the land they longed for. When Moses and Aaron and Caleb and Joshua tried to persuade the people to remember the Lord's faithfulness and His power on their behalf, the people were so far gone that they wanted to stone the men who believed God. These people absolutely refused to believe. They barely seemed to believe *in* God, but they certainly and steadfastly refused to *believe* God. And God took it personally.

Once again, as at Mount Sinai, God pledged to destroy the current crop of Israelites, and once again Moses persuaded Him to forgive them instead. Moses certainly couldn't tout the people's good character, but he did extol the goodness of God's character. However, the justice of God, including His divine right to judge disobedience and rebellion, would now roll over Israel, not unlike it had done against Egypt. Love and justice, the two parts of His nature that might appear to war against each other (though they are not really dissimilar), are reflected in the words He spoke to Moses in Numbers 14:20–23: "I have forgiven them, as you asked. Nevertheless, as surely as I live and as surely as the glory of the LORD fills the whole earth, not one of the men who *saw* my glory and the miraculous signs I performed in Egypt and in the desert but who disobeyed me and tested me ten times—not one of them will ever see the land I promised on oath to their forefathers. No one who has *treated me with contempt* will ever see it." The insurrectionists were forgiven by God. *Nevertheless,* they could not be excused from their unbelief. Those who *witness* the greatness of God and *refuse to believe* will pay a great price.

> *Those who witness the greatness of God and refuse to believe will pay a great price.*

SAME SONG, SECOND VERSE; COULD GET BETTER, BUT IT'S GONNA GET WORSE

The disbelieving and disobedient Israelites were sentenced to wander in the wilderness for forty years, one year for every day they explored the abundance of what God offered and they rejected, until every one of the rebellious, contemptuous adults died. Among the Israelites age twenty and older, only Joshua and Caleb, who believed "wholeheartedly" (how God honors the heart that truly belongs to Him!), would survive the journey back to Canaan. Numbers 14:34 contains some of the most frightening words in Scripture. God told His people, those chosen for His holy purpose, that there is a high price to pay for rebellion. "You will suffer for your sins and"—here come the words—"[you will] know what it is like to have me against you." These were breathtaking words from the Holy God, who had in such varied and visible ways been completely *for* them. I can't imagine the fear and dread that would envelope me to know that God was going to act *against* me. What worse fate could befall a child of God? It was not His choice to turn His back until they determinedly and repeatedly turned theirs. They refused to see Him. They refused to believe Him. Now He would refuse to spare them.

For forty years the chosen people wandered in the desert. Stiff-necked, self-centered rebellion turned an eleven-day trip from Sinai to Canaan into a forty-year tour of the wilderness. Those must have been bleak years as one by one people dropped and died, perished in battles, or were struck dead by God for further rebellion. During the forty years there were confrontations with various cousins such as the Edomites (from Esau) and the Moabites (from Lot), and there were skirmishes with future neighbors. There was more grumbling against God (What was it going to take to persuade them this was not a good idea?), which one time was judged by poisonous snakes. There was one event with a talking donkey, which the Israelites didn't actually witness but which shows that God can use even a dumb animal to proclaim smart advice.

And then there was the incident that changed Moses' destination from the Promised Land to heaven. I don't understand how he kept from losing his temper much earlier. I would have been sorely and frequently tempted to strike a few people down with my staff had I been the leader of Israel. (I'm pretty sure that's why churches don't issue staffs to their shepherds!) But when Moses finally lost it, he lost a great deal.

TWO STRIKES, AND YOU'RE NOT IN

One day, in the midst of another episode of ungrateful people grumbling because some previously visited springs had gone dry, Moses made a costly mistake. God told him to speak to the rock he had struck before, and the Provider would produce water again. In frustration, Moses said, "Listen, you rebels, must we bring you water out of this rock?" and struck the rock twice, thereby intimating that his own effort was saving the people. Moses was to speak and let God get the credit for salvation. Instead, he struck the rock as if his own powerful staff would accomplish the deed. God considered Moses' actions a lack of trust and even a rebellion against His holiness and His right to provide for His people.

To our way of thinking, the judgment against Moses seems a little harsh after all he had been through and after all the times he had persuaded God not to strike the people down, but Moses' position as God's representative before the people demanded that he be judged by a higher standard. (This brings to mind the warning given in James 3:1 for anyone who has assumed the authority to speak for God.) By the way, would I be a rebel (again) to say perhaps God was doing Moses a huge favor when He informed him that he would be denied entry to Canaan with a bunch of griping people? Instead, Moses would very soon enter heaven, where God is and where grumbling people are scarce as hen's teeth. Where's the bad part of that deal?

I don't think Moses knew at the time that his imminent reward was going to far exceed what the Promised Land on earth could offer. He surely was dismayed that he would not pass over into the land that God had long held out as the reward for ending a very long trek through physical and spiritual desert. But believing, faithful, and loyal to the very end, even knowing that the much-desired reward of the Promised Land would not be his, Moses remained with the people of God until He led them all back to the door of promise once more.

FAMOUS LAST WORDS

I always ask my students what Moses did to prepare the new generation to go bravely into the land their parents had feared too much to enter. Did he teach them sword skills, karate, foreign languages? No, he preached. In fact, almost the entire book of Deuteronomy is made up of three "sermons" Moses preached on the border of the Promised Land. In his message to the people of God, Moses extolled the Lord, *their* God. He taught them about the God who had been with them from the beginning and would continue to be with them until the end. He told them about the God who was the overseer of all passages, whether *from* Egypt, *through* the wilderness, or *into* the Promised Land.

The chosen people gathered for Moses' final message. A very old man stood before a new generation of Israelites. At least twice as old as the oldest among them, Moses reached out to these "new" people of God with a reminder of who God was and what that meant for them. He took them back through their history and the heritage that had shaped them. He spoke of bondage and the Deliverer. He reminded them of the Law and the Giver of the Law. He talked of the guiding presence of the Almighty among them. He brought to their recollection the care and concern the Lord showed for them every day of their lives by feeding them and healing them and loving them. He spoke of the necessity for obedience to the God who ruled from above. He had a simple theme: God did it all. He had a simple message: Remember!

Moses spoke to people who couldn't recall the enticing pleasures of Egypt, yet he knew that the allure of a place *like* Egypt was still deep in their hearts. He warned, "Only be careful, and watch yourselves closely so that you do not forget the things your eyes have seen or let them slip from your heart as long as you live. Teach them to your children and to their children after them." Then hammering on a theme he knew defined humanity itself, Moses pleaded, "When you have eaten and are satisfied, praise the Lord your God for the good land he has given you. Be careful that you do not forget the Lord your God.... Otherwise, when you eat and are satisfied, when you build fine houses and settle down, when your [possessions] grow large and your [riches] increase and all you have is multiplied, then your heart will become proud and you will forget the Lord your God.... You may say to yourself, 'My power and the strength of my hands have produced this wealth for me.' But *remember* the Lord your God, for it is he who gives."

Moses certainly knew his audience. The time would come way too soon when every scenario he spoke of would play itself out. In spite of some of the sternest, most graphic and fearsome descriptions in Scripture of where disobedience would lead, God's children would disobey their God. Too soon the people would ignore who God is. Too soon they would forget what God had done. Too soon the fleshly nature of humanity would crowd out the spiritual. And along with it, the spirited and Spirit-filled words God's great man spoke in those days would be disregarded as well.

Still, Moses' words remain for all God's children in all times who really want to know what God wants. Read those words. The first four books of the Bible (also penned by Moses) tell of God choosing man. Deuteronomy speaks of the necessity for man to *choose God.* The words recorded there renew the Law, review the sacrifices, and repeatedly emphasize God's demand for obedience. But they also call for *relationship* and punctuate the Lord's desire that *love* be the motivation for obedience and that a *heart* is the truest offering His child can bring Him. Moses' final words are some of the most quoted words in the New Testament, especially by our Lord Christ Himself. They are God-breathed and reflective of the very heart of Almighty God.

Then, after speaking some of the greatest words ever spoken, Moses—maybe the greatest human servant ever called by the Lord—went to face God. At the age of 120, "his eyes were not weak nor his strength gone." Moses climbed up Mount Nebo, where his Lord was waiting for him. The Lord showed Moses the whole land that would be given to the people he had led there, and together, a servant and his Master, a leader and his Guide, a man and his God viewed the Promised Land.

In His final act of love for Moses, God took him to a place far exceeding the destination he had sought. God took Moses home. And somewhere only He would ever know, God himself buried the body of the man who had loved and served Him faithfully for so long and through so much.

And then God turned His eyes toward the Promised Land and the people to whom He had promised it.

11 MOVE IN, MOVE ON

A NEW LAND

Who is this King of glory?
The LORD strong and mighty,
the LORD mighty in battle.

—PSALM 24:8

JOSHUA

I have a friend who likes to walk around in cemeteries and read tombstones. While it wouldn't be my first choice of how to spend a free afternoon, you can learn a lot about people by how others sum up their lives. If Moses had been given a headstone, his epitaph would surely have read: "No prophet has risen in Israel like Moses, whom the LORD knew face to face, who did all those miraculous signs and wonders the LORD sent him to do in Egypt . . . For no one has ever shown the mighty power or performed the awesome deeds that Moses did in the sight of all Israel."

That was quite a legacy to leave. Moses was also quite a hard act to follow. For forty years he had schlepped a couple of million feuding, feckless, and faithless people through the wilderness up to the door of the Promised Land . . . twice! He had been a visible leader, lawgiver, and mediator for all those years. What would they do without him? When the "parent" was no longer around, would the "children" remain faithful?

The Israelites found themselves at the door of Promise, and they found themselves well provisioned (with miracle food) and well protected (by a marvelous God).

Their shoes and clothes had not worn out after forty years of walking. Miracles—and Moses—had gotten them to the place where they now stood: at the border of Canaan with a raging river in front of them. Who would lead them over the river (and through the woods)? You can rest assured it would be the same leader they'd always had. God was going to lead them over, into, and through their new world. It had always been God who had led them. He would soon make it abundantly clear to them that He still did.

It would also become abundantly clear that God had chosen the right man to replace Moses. Before Moses died, he prayed for a leader "to go out and come in before them, one who will lead them out and bring them in, so the Lord's people will not be like sheep without a shepherd." And in answer to Moses' prayer, God had him lay hands on his replacement in front of the whole assembly so they would know God was with the new leader too. So Moses, "as the LORD instructed," commissioned one of God's most faithful followers to follow him as Israel's point man.

JOSHUA, FIT FOR BATTLE

Joshua was a descendant of Joseph, from the tribe of Ephraim. The name, which comes from the same root word as "Jesus" in Greek, means "Jehovah saves," and Joshua's life would exhibit that he believed it. He was born in slavery in Egypt and recognized that he had been led out by the Almighty's gracious hand. A beholder of God's wonders for more than forty years, Joshua was a true devotee. He had been Moses' trusted aide and an eyewitness to a leader who had followed and the God who had led. Since he had accompanied Moses part of the way up Mount Sinai, Joshua had not participated in the idolatry of the golden calf and therefore had remained a pure worshiper of the true God. He, like Caleb, had seen God's bounty in the Promised Land and had believed God's power over its inhabitants. As the valiant captain of Israel's army, Joshua knew how to fight, and he trusted that any army God led would surely be victorious. Joshua had two hard jobs ahead of him: he had to take over for God's greatest leader, and he had to take the Promised Land for God. But he had two things going for him as well: he knew whom he led, and he knew whom he followed.

Have you ever wondered what it was like to be Joshua? To me, he is one of the most admirable men in all of Scripture. It wasn't simply because he had good training, impressive skills, and stellar character—all of which he possessed in abundance.

It was because he had to step into some very big shoes. God Himself had said there was no one like Moses. Even the people of Israel had to be a little uneasy with Moses gone. Yet Joshua, with one of the greatest displays of humility in Scripture, walked out of the shadow of the greatest character in the Old Testament and, using his own gifts, devoted his life to the Lord and the Lord's people.

Have you ever taken over a job from someone who was really good and really loved? You have only a few choices in how to proceed. You can try to out-Moses your Moses. Or you can give up in despair because you can never measure up. Or you can be like Joshua. You can be the very best Joshua you can be and let God mold you into what He needs.

Once the call and the commission were issued to Joshua and the people had time to mourn the passing of Moses, the Lord commanded Joshua to equip Israel for its own passage. He told him to prepare to cross over and get ready to receive. God wanted His people to know that they were about to receive the land He was anxious to give them. He also wanted them to believe it would happen just as He had promised. "I will give you every place where you set your foot, as I promised Moses. . . . No one will be able to stand up against you all the days of your life. As I was with Moses, so I will be with you; I will never leave you nor forsake you." In the same words with which God issued Joshua his marching orders, He assured him that He would march before him. Joshua and Israel would never be without the provision and the protection of the Promise-keeper, who was about to deliver on the first promise He had given to Abraham and his descendants all those years ago: a land to call their own.

God had a few words specifically for Israel's new leader. Three times God told him to "be strong and courageous," once even adding "*very* courageous." Why? Because God certainly knew the fortitude it took to lead these people. The inhabitants of the land would not welcome them or the ways of their God, and Israel would need a leader who knew God's will, was committed to follow God's way, and would never deviate from obedience to God's law. God's final "be strong and courageous" came as a *command* to Joshua. He accompanied it by saying, "Do not be terrified; do not

During hard times we are tempted to give in to fear and dread. And how do we combat that temptation? We remember. I am with you.

be discouraged." Why so emphatic? Because God knows the human heart. During frightening events, during hard times, during long ordeals, we are tempted to give in to fear and dread. And how do we combat that temptation? We remember. God reminded Joshua of the one thing he needed to remember in the mission ahead: I AM *with* you.

So Joshua believed, and he prepared. He told the people that in three days they would cross over into the land God would give them. This new leader certainly wasn't wasting time! To find out what he would face, the good general and former spy sent two scouts to check out the land, "especially Jericho." Being the military tactician he was, Joshua knew he would need to take out the bully on the block first. It was a strategic move to gain control of the passage into the land, a passage that Jericho occupied. And it was a warning shot to the rest of the inhabitants that a powerful new force was moving in.

ON THE JERICHO ROAD

The first place the spies went was to the house of Rahab, a prostitute who lived in a home on the wall surrounding Jericho. I know that some people, especially women, have tried to deny or at least downplay Rahab's profession because it sounds so bad. (I remember the scandalous questions it evoked in my youth, and it is still quite a challenge to explain to fifth graders!) However, the Scriptures rarely refer to her without a tag line accompanying her name: "Rahab, the prostitute." I think her profession is what makes her actions regarding the spies so admirable, and it is her profession that makes God's actions and attitude toward her so marvelous.

Don't you imagine God directed the spies to the house of Rahab? True, the men of the city probably gathered there, so it would be a good place to gather information to take back to Joshua. And true, if the spies were spotted, its location on the wall could provide a quick escape (which they were, and it did). But I'm convinced that God directed the men to Rahab's house so they could meet Rahab and hear what she had to say. God used a pagan woman's expression of belief in Israel's God to further convince Israel that their God was just who He claimed to be. She told them, "I know that the LORD has given this land to you," and she called Him by name: "the LORD." She had heard what God had done at the Red Sea to deliver His people and how He had defeated their enemies along the way to Canaan, and she knew He was going to deliver her land to those who were claiming it for God. She even acknowledged God's right to do so when she said, "For the LORD your God *is* God in heaven above and on earth below."

When I got to this place in the story several years ago with my fifth-grade class, one of my students decided to make the point of the story for me, even though he had no idea that was what he was doing. Bradley was one of those kids who had something to say about everything. In fact, he never stopped talking, even when I was talking. But sometimes he surprised everyone, especially me, with his "out of the mouths of babes" wisdom. As I was extolling the virtues of Rahab's words to the two spies, Bradley shouted out, "Isn't that amazing!" In spite of knowing it could be dangerous, I asked him exactly what amazed him. And he replied with all his eleven-year-old enthusiasm, "God's enemies believed in God when His own people didn't!" Bradley had just nailed it—the big reason, I'm convinced, that God sent his spies to the home of Rahab, a pagan woman of ill repute who believed.

The Israelites really needed to hear the report brought back by the two spies. God had already made a miraculous impact upon the people who then inhabited the Promised Land. Though the early Israelites had seen God's power with their own eyes, they hadn't believed He could conquer the Promised Land the first time. But, inside the land, the inhabitants who had merely *heard* what the Lord had done quaked fearfully in their *conviction* that He could do it this time. Forty years after the failure of Israel's memory, Jericho remembered! (Do you think the reports of what happened came directly from Egypt, who reportedly considered Canaan one of its provinces? It might explain why the Egyptians, still a world power, never interfered with Israel's invasion. Just imagine the reports Egypt could have sent to Canaan regarding what they remembered about Israel's God!)

As for Rahab, in addition to gaining a prominent place in the story of Jericho, she gained a place in the heart of God. She threw herself on His mercy to save her and her family when He conquered the city. And when everything else in Jericho perished, she displayed her faith by displaying the same rope with which she had spared the spies from capture. And in faith, she and her family were spared by God. God accepted one we would have rejected because of who she was. In fact, God honored her. She would later marry a man from the tribe of Judah by the name of Salmon and give birth to a son they would name Boaz. He would have a son named Obed, who would have a son named Jesse, who would have a son named David! All of which makes Rahab, by my calculations, the great-great-grandmother of God's greatest king. And it puts her right in the lineage of the King of kings! Isn't God great!

The report the spies took back to Joshua was good news for Israel. And there was some good news *from* Israel as well. They seemed to have learned something vital during the four decades living out the Lord's justice. The two spies Joshua sent into Canaan came back with a very different report than the group who had gone in with him forty years before: "The LORD has surely given the whole land into our hands; all the people are melting in fear because of us." A few words point out their renewed faith: "*The LORD* . . . has *surely* . . . *given* . . . the *whole* land into our hands; *all* the people are melting in fear because of us." That's quite a conversion story! Those words reflect a giant step in faith. However, when my kids read this passage and locate the words of faith, I also ask if they can identify any word that indicates a potential concern. It may take a few clues, but then the small word *us* pops out. It's a bit worrisome that the spies declared the people of Canaan were melting in fear because of "us." I really wish they had gone all the way and said the hearts were melting in fear because of "our God."

STEP OUT, STEP UP

Three days after receiving the spies' account, Joshua prepared the people to cross into Canaan. Two miraculous crossings marked Israel's passage to promise. One had been a passage from sin (the escape from Egypt's hold). The other would be a passage to safety (entry into God's promised rest). God was in control of both. Of the Israelites still alive, only Joshua and Caleb recalled the first memorable passage. It seems that God wanted everyone else to have something memorable as well. So Joshua sent his officers to spread the word that when the people saw the ark of the covenant move out, they were to follow it. The ark represented the presence of God, the place "under His wings," so to speak. God's very presence would guide His people as they headed into the land. But first they needed to consecrate themselves for such an awesome occurrence. They needed to be purified in order to be in God's presence, and they needed to be ready to join His procession when God manifested that presence among them to lead them over. Then Joshua told them to get ready to see God, "for tomorrow the LORD will do amazing things among you."

After declaring what God intended to do—to divide the waters of the Jordan River when the priests carrying the ark stepped into it—Joshua ordered, at God's command, that the people memorialize the passage. He told them to gather twelve stones, one for each tribe, from the middle of the Jordan River, right where the priests would stand, and carry them to the other side. The stones were to be set up at their camp in their new land to serve as a reminder forever of the passage into promise. ("Remember!") The people were instructed to display the stones "to serve as a sign among you," and in the future when their children who had not witnessed the crossing would ask what the twelve standing stones meant, the parents were to "tell them." Why is it important to remember? Why is it important to tell? The answer is given in Joshua 4:24: "so that all the peoples of the earth might know that the hand of the LORD is powerful and so that you might always fear the LORD your God." God always had a message for His own people when He sent a message to others. His children in all times are to know who God is and remember what He can do. And we are all to live like we believe it so others can know Him as well.

> *His children in all times are to know who God is and remember what He can do. And we are all to live like we believe it so others can know Him as well.*

I like the image of a stone of remembrance—a touchstone, so to speak. It's good to reconnect with a special event or place or maybe a special time in the past that had a profound impact on your life: returning to the family farm, going back for the fiftieth anniversary of the church where you grew up, taking your mother and aunt on a drive around their old haunts while listening to their stories of a time long gone.

Or maybe your stone of remembrance is something like mine—a defining event that forever changed your life and reshaped your outlook on life, a time that brought you face to face with who you are and face to face with God. The week between Christmas and New Year's in 1988 was the beginning of a saga that would alter my family forever. My then fifteen-year-old son was diagnosed with cancer, and his diagnosis and treatment dominated the next three years of our lives. It was like the introduction to *A Tale of Two Cities:* it was the best of times; it was the worst of times. Through the bleakest days and the darkest nights, we existed in fear and fatigue. It was grueling.

It was all consuming. It could have destroyed us. Instead, just as God promises in 1 Peter 1:6–7, it made us better. We learned the meaning of sacrifice. We found out how much we loved each other. We met a God in heaven who we discovered could sustain us in the worst that life could throw at us. I personally moved from a textbook belief in God to a lifestyle faith in Him.

My son was home from college one weekend several years later, and I can clearly see him hoisting himself onto the kitchen counter and saying to me, "I know you're going to think this is strange, but there are a lot of things I miss about those days." I told him that I completely understood. In the worst days of our lives we learned what really matters, who really cares, and to Whom we can absolutely entrust our futures. When we remember what God has done for us and in us, we can truly believe He will continue to be faithful.

God will always demonstrate His love and His great faithfulness to each generation that remembers.

I really hope that the Israelite children who came along later and saw the stones of remembrance received both information and inspiration when the witnesses to God's care told them of all they had seen. It's hard to imagine anything more rewarding than passing on to the next generation the assurance that the same God who cared for your ancestors cares just as much for you. God will always demonstrate His love and His great faithfulness to each generation that remembers.

After the twelve men gathered the stones of remembrance, the Israelites passed through the Jordan River and into the Promised Land. A few facts make that passage especially interesting. The Jordan River is different from most rivers. It is not considered sacred, nor is it a commercial river for travel or transporting goods, nor does it have a fertile delta for growing crops. It is not a broad river, being only fifty to seventy-five feet at its widest, but it is not easy to cross. The Jordan apparently flows through a rift in the earth's crust and is mostly a crevice with a steep drop-off rather than a gentle slope. At flood stage, which we are specifically told was the case when the Israelites crossed the Jordan, the first step into the water could possibly have been over the priests' heads. So those priests who took that first step into the river really made a leap of faith.

I'm reminded of the scene in *Indiana Jones and the Last Crusade* when the crusader stood on the precipice of a bottomless chasm, knowing his next step toward his goal was described as a leap of faith. Finally he stuck out his leg over that void and put his foot firmly down on a path that appeared only when he trusted it to be there. When I saw the movie, I recognized the significance of that scene, and it has been burned in my memory ever since. It took me quite a few years to give the same credit to the priests' faith as to Indiana Jones's. But those priests had no reason to believe that solid ground would open up under their feet except their trust in the God who promised it would.

There is another interesting thing about the Jordan River. References in Scripture and song nearly always present the Jordan as a barrier of sorts, one that the people of God must cross in order to receive something better. It is used as a symbol of death, and passing over it leads to a better life. It was the scene of Jesus' baptism and the beginning of His public ministry and message that pointed to a better way of living. The Jordan River now stood as a barrier between the weary Israelites and the land that promised them rest from their journey. But nothing would happen until they stepped out in faith. And when they stepped out in faith, God removed the barrier, and all His people passed over. As they passed over, they passed alongside God. They could see His presence in the ark that stood in the middle of the crossing, in the dry ground beneath their feet, and in the land in front of them that flowed with His promise of milk and honey.

THIS LAND IS YOUR LAND, THIS LAND IS MY LAND

Once inside the land, God ordered steps to be taken that would remind His people of who they were and who their God was. All the men had to be circumcised as the covenant sign of being set apart for God, a practice that had been neglected during the wilderness years. It was, in a sense, an excising of the old life they had been living. Next the people celebrated Passover. How appropriate was the timing! And then the day after eating their Passover meal, the people partook of the bounty of the land God was giving them. "Taste and see that the LORD is good." And the day after they ate Canaan's bread, the manna, their bread of heaven that had fed them for forty years, ceased. God's provision for them would now come from the land they were about to inherit.

Inheritance—a bequest, estate, endowment, something one *receives*. It is not earned and often not deserved. It comes through someone else's hard work or good will. These Israelites were about to be *given* a land with large, flourishing cities they did not build, homes filled with things they did not provide, wells they did not dig, vineyards and olive groves they did not plant. The words of Moses and Joshua ring in our ears as we imagine what God was placing in their hands. It's the very image of what we are bound for in God's Promised Land. It's the provision He offers those of us who know that the wilderness we now inhabit is not our home, that the journey we are currently on will lead us to something far better than we can ask or even imagine.

God was giving this good land into the hands of His children, but He also required that they take it. And the biggest, baddest city of them all—Jericho—stood right in their path. The ancient, walled city protected the entrance into the heart of Canaan. Because of its walls, an assault was virtually impossible. It would have been a challenge to professional soldiers, and Israel's army was made up mostly of shepherds. With what strategy could Joshua wage a successful campaign against the strongest fortress he had ever faced in battle?

The plan was taken out of Joshua's hands when he met a man near Jericho who introduced himself as the commander of the Lord's army. And Joshua hit the dirt! Then he replied with the same humility that marked all God's greatest men: "What message does *my Lord* have for *his servant*?" The commander of the Lord's army replied, "Take off your sandals, for the place where you are standing is holy." And Joshua did. He may not have fully realized who was usurping his leadership in the coming battle, but he certainly realized from Whom he had come. That day Joshua met a representative of God himself. Whether he was God in human form (a pre-manifestation of Christ, some scholars believe—after all, holy ground indicates the presence of God) or whether he was an angel of superior rank, Joshua recognized that God was going to be his general in the coming conflict. I love this story, as Joshua for the first time fully realized that the army of Israel was indeed God's, not his own. It's also likely that he didn't realize Israel's army wouldn't be the only army going into battle against Jericho. Whatever he believed, with his acquiescence to the Lord Almighty's leadership, Joshua received plans for the strangest battle that would ever be fought.

It's hard to imagine what went through the minds of everyone involved in the battle of Jericho. The old song proclaims that Joshua "fit" the battle, but the battle was fought by a force far greater than Joshua's could ever be. Jericho was tightly shut up, prepared for a siege. When the "assault" came, it was totally unprecedented. The armed men of Israel accompanied front and rear what appeared to be the heart of the procession of warriors. What's going on here? Is that the marching band with their trumpets? And what is that gold box they're carrying? Where are the battering rams, the catapults? Where's their armor? What kind of a battle is this? Did even the Israelites wonder about their general's sanity when they received their orders? Did Jericho quake in fear, wait in dread, or after a few days snicker that the stories they had heard about these people and their God must have been exaggerated or even fabricated? Whatever all the participants thought, on the seventh day of "battle" when the trumpets sounded and the people shouted and the walls fell, all doubt was removed about who was moving into Canaan.

Was it good vibrations? Was it weak foundations? Or did the walls of Jericho fall by angel breath? That's what I think. I believe it was the same invisible army of horses and flaming chariots that would later surround Elisha. And when God's people, at God's command, shouted with the voice of faith in God's salvation, the commander of God's army and his host blew the walls of Jericho flat!

MORE THAN CONQUEROR

Only one small glitch slowed down Joshua's assault on Canaan after that. God dealt immediately and vividly with one who ignored His command to take nothing from Jericho for self but to leave everything for God, who had won the battle. The Almighty's demonstration of intolerance for sin in the camp was enough to impel His people to a fairly quick conquest of the land. Joshua's strategy—to cut Canaan in half and separate the north from the south, to execute quick ambushes, to march his army at night and rely on the element of surprise, and throw in a "small assist" from God, who made the sun stand still for one mop-up operation—accomplished the goal of subjugating the Promised Land in just a few years.

After Joshua's campaign through Canaan was completed, he was an old man. Not all the land was cleared of inhabitants as God had directed, but each tribe would be responsible for cleaning out its own territory when it took possession. Joshua spent the final years of his life dispensing the land to the individual tribes, setting up cities of refuge and Levitical locations, and governing the people of God. As he reached the end of his life, he was tired and ready to die. (Have you ever noticed that

God's hardest workers are always the most ready to die?) But before Joshua died, he called all Israel together to hear his parting words.

Like his predecessor, Joshua started out by reminding the people of God about God. "You yourselves have seen everything the LORD your God has done to all these nations for your sake; it was the LORD your God who fought for you." Remember! *Remember* what God has done! *Trust* what God will do! Be very careful to *love* the Lord your God.

He promised them that if they held fast to God, served Him, obeyed Him completely, worshiped Him only, the same God who had driven out their enemies before them would empower them to drive out their remaining enemies. Joshua urged the Israelites to obey all the Lord had commanded, not to use their imaginations or make executive decisions regarding the Lord's will for them. The Israelites would have been well served to remember his words.

The old man continued by admonishing the people of God not to fraternize with their neighbors. He warned them that if they entangled themselves with the evil people around them in marriage or alliances or even as neighbors, their God would not drive out the enemies. Instead, their new "friends" would ensnare them, enslave them, and finally cause them to be erased from the land.

Joshua warned Israel to have nothing to do with the terrible gods of the Canaanites: not to call on their names for help, not to depend on them for anything, not to serve them, not to worship them.

And Joshua wrapped it up by telling God's people that they would *choose* the way they would go. It was the same free will God had established in the beginning with the inhabitants of the garden, that first land of milk and honey. The choice belonged to the people. It's that heart thing again. Mankind must decide whom to believe and whose will to follow. Joshua urged the people of God to choose God: "Choose for yourselves this day whom you will serve, whether the gods your forefathers served beyond the River, or the gods of the Amorites, in whose land you are living." Don't hesitate. Don't vacillate. Decide today where your loyalty lies. Decide to whom your heart belongs. Joshua knew whom he had chosen. He and his household would choose the One who had chosen him.

It is a warning to all God's children . . . Israel meant to be faithful!

The people were convicted by Joshua's fervent words, and they answered back, "Far be it from us to forsake the LORD to serve other gods!" (Yeah, and while the mountain of God was still smoking with His presence, His people would never build a calf god!) As the voice of Joshua died away, the Israelites proclaimed, "We too will serve the LORD, because he is our God." And they meant it. Beware! It is a warning to all God's children . . . Israel *meant* to be faithful!

And for a while, they were. As long as those who knew Joshua were still alive, the people remained faithful. They remembered.

12 Disorder in the Court
The Judges

They would not listen to their judges
but prostituted themselves to other gods and worshiped them.
Unlike their fathers, they quickly turned from the way
in which their fathers had walked,
the way of obedience to the LORD's commands.

—JUDGES 2:17

JUDGES–RUTH

Are you the type of person who finds it more difficult to "remain" than to "become"? I am. I'm rather project oriented, and I don't do very well with maintenance. I've talked to many women who have dieted, and most agree it was easier to lose weight than it was to maintain their weight loss. The moment a dieter starts feeling really deprived of her favorite foods and begins to fret that she will never get to eat them again, she can talk herself into a reward for her previous good behavior and gradually fall back into the bad habits that first led to weight gain. Likewise, for some it is easier to get organized than it is to keep things in order, especially if one is, by nature, disorderly. And while a one-time cleanup is hard, it is still easier than maintaining cleanliness, because that is never ending and demands constant attention. Maintaining is difficult, especially if you're going against your innate inclination. It takes an act of will and real character to overcome the "natural" person.

Joshua was the real thing. Unfortunately, the people who followed him proved unable to sustain the standard he set, and before long they set out in a different direction than the way he had led. Once they started down their own path, it became a slippery slope to sin.

A BRAVE NEW WORLD WITH BAD OLD WAYS

God had commanded His people to clear out the inhabitants of Canaan (lots of "-ites"). Their land was infested with some really bad old ways and some really bad gods. Baal, the principal god of Canaan, was worshiped as the god of weather, war, and fertility, among other things, and his "wife," Ashtoreth, was the goddess of reproduction. The priestesses were temple prostitutes and sodomites, and their worship involved sexual orgies. (Wouldn't you love to explain this to fifth graders?) Chemosh, the god of the Moabites (from Lot), was worshiped by human sacrifice, and Molech, another god of the Canaanites (from cousin Ham), was appeased by the burning of children. The worship of the local gods involved debauchery on every level. Moses had warned the people to "be careful not to be ensnared by inquiring about their gods. . . . They do all kinds of detestable things the LORD hates. They even burn their sons and daughters in the fire as sacrifices to their gods." The lives, the gods, and the worship of the people of Canaan were abhorrent to Holy God. Why do you think He wanted them cleared out?

Because He knows! He knows how easy it is to compromise . . . to go along in order to get along. He knows how we desire approval from those around us. We will compromise our standards, if necessary, to impress those we want to impress. And ultimately, even without intending to, we become indistinguishable from those around us.

What was Israel's purpose as a people? To *be holy* in an unholy world. God intended for His people to control the land in which He had placed them, because He had a purpose in placing them there. Canaan was at a crossroads of the world. Through their territory ran major trade routes, north to south and east to west. Imagine this: the Promised Land was not the ultimate goal of the Israelites. Influencing those who

> *The Promised Land was not the ultimate goal of the Israelites. Influencing those who passed through their land was.*

passed through their land was. That's why sin had to be purged from the camp. That's why evil influences had to be driven out from among them. God's people had a world to influence for God!

Unfortunately, rather than following through on God's instructions and their own good intentions, the Israelites didn't completely purge the land. Instead, they got weary of battling those around them. They decided to "live and let live." (After all, what right does anyone have to inflict his beliefs on others?) The people of God settled down among the Canaanites and began to think, *Oh, they're not so bad . . .* They let their children play with Canaanite children. They began to notice that the Canaanite women were pretty fine looking. They began to hedge their bets with fertility gods and crop gods—just to supplement Jehovah's power, not replace Him . . . just to avoid putting all their eggs in one basket! And less than fifty years after Joshua's death, God's people—despite the purpose they'd been given and the vow they'd sworn—were virtually indistinguishable from those around them. They "prostituted themselves to other gods and worshiped them." God's holy people were *in* the land God had given them, and they had rather quickly become *of* the land as well.

LIKE A CYCLE IN A CYCLE

It was not really a *nation* that inhabited the land of Canaan. Well, technically it was, because they spoke the same language, had the same ethnicity, and even had a system of laws that supposedly governed them. But the times right after settling the Promised Land remind me of the early confederation of states before our nation became the United States of America. Each tribe was somewhat independent of the others, autonomous, with no central government. There was no union (except for their common religion, which was weakened by compromise), nor was there a great deal of unity. They had a type of treaty with each other, a "lean on me when you're not strong" agreement to help each other out in case of attack by someone else. But otherwise they were more a "you're not the boss of me" kind of coalition. One verse sums up the times well: "In those days Israel had no king; everyone did as he saw fit."

What happens when there are a lot of small settlements with enemies living around and among them? Well, it's fairly easy for those enemies, who have been displaced from home and are up in arms about it, to pick off the settlements one by one.

And that's what happened to the tribes of Israel in Canaan. They were usurpers who lived among enemies. And they were ripe for the picking!

Consequently, Israel entered a bleak time in its history. The people were morally and politically weak, and they began a cycle that would spiral down into corruption and degradation. Because of their sin, God allowed the enemies around them—those people they had tried to accommodate and finally to emulate—to judge Israel for its disobedience. The tribes were bedeviled and afflicted, and sometimes even subjugated, by the outsiders inside and around their land. Their lives became miserable as God turned His back on those who had rejected Him.

Finally, in the midst of despair and desperation, someone would remember they had a God who cared about them. Then they would call on God to save them. And—marvel in the awesomeness of God's love—He would do it. He would raise up a special leader for the catastrophe at hand, and He would use that judge to deliver God's justice against the enemies of the chosen. Then His people would praise their God for His salvation, and they would live at ease in the land again.

The book of Judges might have been really short if the people could have maintained their faithfulness, but after a time of peace that would follow God's victory, the people would drift again. They would forget again. They would try to find a happy medium with their neighbors again. They would again prostitute themselves with the wicked gods of the wicked people around them, and pretty soon the vicious cycle would start all over. Time after time they repeated the cycle of sin, subjugation, and salvation, followed by more sin. It was really ugly.

But it is really interesting to teach. (I hesitate to say "fun," but with kids' general enjoyment of gruesome subject matter, the book of Judges is "fun" to teach.)

THE GOOD, THE BAD, AND THE STUDLY

The stories of the twelve warrior judges are among my kids' favorites to study. The 350 years covered in the book of Judges include vivid tales of colorful characters. From the account of left-handed Ehud meeting morbidly obese Eglon in the tale of the disappearing sword to the Philistine philandering of Samson, the book is chock-full of some of the most bloodcurdling, cringe-inducing stories to be found outside the fairy tales we read to our children before we put them down for a peaceful night's sleep!

Deborah, a feminine female in a manly and patriarchal system, was accepted as a prophetess, a writer of songs, and the leader of her tribe in all things judicial. She even agreed to accompany Barak, the commander of the army, into battle when he refused to go without her. She was a feminist's dream.

But the sisters must really relish the story of Jael, who "brought the battle to a head" when she nailed the enemy general Sisera through the temple with a tent peg! (One of my friends once taught this story and entitled it "Baal, Hail, Jael, and the Nail." I love a good synopsis!)

The reluctant judge, Gideon, made a couple of sheepish moves with some fleece before he accepted God's invitation to mix it up with the Midianites, and then learned all about downsizing to demonstrate the bigness of God. With only three hundred men who lapped up the chance to go into battle against armed thousands while using just ancient flashlights, musical instruments, and crockery as weapons, Gideon proved that weakness could be made strong when God is in charge and obedience is in place.

> *Gideon proved that weakness could be made strong when God is in charge and obedience is in place.*

To wrap up the study of the judges, sing it with me . . .

You know Othniel and Ehud and Shamgar and Deborah.
Gideon and Tola and Jephthah and Jair.
But do you recall the most famous judge of them all?

(I kind of want to keep singing, "Samson, the red-faced, reigned, dear," but I'm afraid it isn't appropriate to be too frivolous here . . .)

Samson, the well-known, weak strongman, was the last of the great warrior judges. He was born out of barrenness and was divinely designed to answer the problem of the Philistines, enemies who had harassed God's chosen for decades. Few individuals have been born with more going for them than Samson. He was prophesied by an angel and, even before his birth, was set apart for excellence. He was ordained to be different from the culture surrounding him, to adopt a unique lifestyle in order to call attention to God's call. Unfortunately, Samson heard other calls: mostly the call of the wild and the song of the siren. I don't believe the man kept a single vow, and I know he never lived up to his potential. The strong man had a pretty hairy existence fighting off the Philistines and chasing after their women, and together the two groups clipped him good. Samson's amazing physical strength was matched only by his astonishing moral weakness. He had the strength to take what he wanted yet lacked the strength to resist what he wanted. In the end, in spite of himself, Samson accomplished what God had called him to do: begin to rescue Israel from the Philistines. But just think what he missed of God along the way.

Few people in the Scriptures give me more pause than does Samson. Every time I read the list of the faithful in Hebrews, I'm actually kind of surprised to find him still listed there. But it also gives me hope to see his name on the same page with the great ones ... because I have far more in common with him than with some of the others. A preacher in my church did a two-sermon miniseries on Samson a few years ago and said something I have never forgotten and have frequently quoted. While talking about this fact that Samson was absolutely ruled by the flesh and yet was listed in Hebrews among the faithful, the preacher said of Samson, "He wasn't *lost*. He was just *less*." How heartbreaking that is when applied to a man who was given everything he needed to be great. And how sobering it is when I think of myself. I am convinced I am not lost from God. But am I less than what He wants me to be?

> *God wants so much more from us than we are willing to give and so much more for us than we are willing to accept.*

I am one who ponders. I like to cogitate, contemplate, cerebrate, and ruminate. And in my ponderings are some wonderings. What does God really want *from* those "he chose . . . before the creation of the world"? Obedience to His way and holy living? Absolutely. Submission of will? Unequivocally. Sacrifice of self? Irrefutably. But is there anything else He wants *for* His children? I'm convinced there is. Jesus claimed that He came so we might live *abundantly*. Unfortunately, I'm not sure we know what that means. We seem too frequently to live our lives *less* than we should: satisfied just to keep the rules, content just to keep the peace, or comfortable even pushing the boundaries of the flesh so grace may abound. But I am persuaded that God wants so much more *from* us than we are willing to give and so much more *for* us than we are willing to accept. Things have not changed since the first call of Abraham. God's people have always been called to live abundant lives to show forth their boundless God. It has been, it is, and it will continue to be our choice whether we will answer the call.

Samson, although a powerful warrior, never fulfilled the call to be all he could have been. Yet God used him in spite of himself—in spite of his weakness, in spite of his willfulness—to begin subjugating the Philistines, the most tenacious inhabitants of the Promised Land. God would later complete that task using a man who was given over heart and soul to the God who called him, thus proving forever what He *really* wants.

The period of the judges ended shortly after Samson's life ended. It was a low point in Israel's history, a time when God "shouldn't" have cared for His people, a time when maybe He "shouldn't" have continued to save His people. But He did . . . anyway. He did because He is God. And, as the God we have come to know and believe, He continues to love and save.

GOOD LOVE IN WOMAN

Maybe it is as proof of God's inexplicable love and His unerring purpose of redemption that the book of Ruth follows the book of Judges in the Bible. Among the hostilities and infidelities, God drops in a little tale of domestic life, an account of faithful love. It is the story of a woman's love for her mother-in-law and a man's love for a woman, and it is eventually the story of God's love for His people. It demonstrates that God cares for gentle things and for individuals and their lives. And it is evidence that His plan to save His people will continue, in spite of people. Quietly, in the book of Ruth, God chose a heathen girl who had a heart He could use, and He made her a bride of one of His true children and an ancestor of His one and only Son. God's grace for people not considered "His own" will most obviously come with His acceptance of the Gentiles in the New Testament, but it was illustrated with His "adoption" of Ruth into His family and into the family whose stories will finish out the Old Testament. At the end of the book of Ruth come the words of the future: Ruth and Boaz had a son they named Obed, who had son named Jesse, who had a son named David.

The book of Ruth begins the saga of David and kings to come. From this point forth, the Old Testament will center mainly on the family of King David as it leads inexorably to the King of kings.

13 A King Is Just Our Thing

King Saul and All

We want a king over us. Then we will be like all the other nations.

—1 Samuel 8:19–20

1 Samuel

I n my efforts to avoid ever having to lead anyone and to excuse my behavior after someone else has had the audacity to take the lead over me, my mantra has always been "I'm not a chief. I'm just a really noisy Indian." I'm not good at making decisions for myself or for any group, but I am frequently a bit too vocal about how things could be done differently or better after a decision has been made. This quality, as you might imagine, makes me really popular with people who are willing to step into a leadership position where I am to be managed. Don't get me wrong; I'm not bragging here. I know it's not an admirable trait but is, in fact, one of my worst. This unpleasant characteristic equates me with the people of Israel as they began to think about who was leading them and how it might be done better.

> *With our God who knows, our God who plans, nothing is uncharted.*

As the days of the judges waned, the people of Israel found themselves in a void of leadership. Behind them were the great patriarchs who had received the promise, the eminent shepherd who had received the Law, the courageous conqueror who had taken the land, and those interim rulers who had accepted God's help time after time. Behind Israel, if they chose to look, was the visible hand of God. Before them lay an unknown future. But if they'd had the right vision of God, they could have rested in this: their future was not uncharted. If we remember nothing else, we must remember that with our God who knows, our God who plans, *nothing* is uncharted.

GOD'S SAM I AM

Into the void of leadership after the warrior judges, God was going to deliver one of His godliest leaders. The plan began in barrenness . . . again. How many of God's "necessary" men (those who proved vital to the implementation of His plan among His people) were born as a gift to a barren mother? Isaac was, and Joseph and Samson. John the Baptist would be. They were born in God's timing, for God's use, to promote God's plan. That is a great description of the man Samuel, whose birth and life open the first book that bears his name.

A baby boy was born in answer to a specific prayer from a surrendered woman. Is surrender to God the secret to successful prayer? Is the prayer that God honors one that acknowledges His sovereignty and His will? Does answered prayer hinge on our submission to and stewardship of God's answers? Hannah's prayer and her response to the Lord's answer is a pretty strong indication that it just might be.

Samuel's name sounds like the Hebrew word for "heard of God." He was born because God heard a woman's prayer, and by the time Samuel was old enough to understand, Hannah made sure her son had *heard of* God and what He had done for her. She knew she had received a son *so* she could give him to God. And when her son was probably three or four years old, barely weaned and housebroken, Hannah took him to the priest to be raised in God's house. The young boy grew up under the guardianship of Eli the priest, but he *grew* under the leadership of Jehovah God. Finally, after more than three hundred years of cyclical sin, God had a man he could use to lead His nation out of darkness, and the man was a child.

The special born child served Eli in the temple, and he lived "in the presence of the LORD." Literally. When God came to call on Samuel to receive the priesthood He was taking from Eli and his wicked sons, God found Samuel "lying down in the temple of the LORD, where the ark of God was." By day Samuel served in the temple, and at night he slept by the ark of God's presence. As was true of his ancestor Joseph (Samuel was from the tribe of Ephraim), "the LORD was with" Samuel. And all of Israel—from Dan to Beersheba, the entire kit and caboodle—soon recognized that was true.

Samuel would hold three offices in Israel. He was the last of the judges to rule the land, to make executive and judicial decisions for the people. He was also a priest who led the people in worship. In both of those positions he replaced Eli, whose sons were corrupt. (As someone once said, they were kind of "priest hoods"!) Although he was crucial as both judge and priest, Samuel's primary position in Israel would be as God's prophet, a spokesman for the Almighty in a world that wasn't particularly interested in hearing what He had to say. Samuel would be the first in a new order of prophets called by God, and he would establish a school of prophets to train the men God would use to speak to His hard-of-hearing children throughout the rest of the Old Testament. Samuel would begin God's restoration of His nation.

REVIVE US AGAIN

The revival in Israel started as many revivals do, as a direct result of recognizing just how far away from God the people had drifted. I think the realization came soon after the Philistines became raiders of the lost ark. One day the Israelites decided to take God to a battle He refused to attend. Demonstrating their ignorance and arrogance in equal parts, they hauled the ark of God's presence into battle, expecting to force Him to fight for them. Give the Israelites credit for recognizing that when God led them in battle, they were victorious, but they

Anytime we try to put God in a box, we have lost touch with who God is.

certainly must be debited for thinking they had God in a box. Anytime we try to put God in a box, we have lost touch with who God is.

As a reminder of how out of touch they were with God and as a result of their presumption against Him, Israel "lost God" in the battle. And the ark, which represented His presence with them, was carried back to the Philistine capital as a trophy to present to their god Dagon or to further supplement the Philistines' many gods. The Israelites had done such a poor job of representing God among the other inhabitants of their world that the Philistines were convinced they could not only *defeat* God but could even *use* Him (somewhat as Israel herself had tried to use Him as a good-luck charm for battle). I love the image as the Philistines placed the captured ark in Dagon's temple and the next morning found the idol facedown before the ark, in the position of a supplicant or worshiper. After righting the statue to his "superior" position, the Philistine priests found Dagon once more facedown, this time with his head and hands broken off—much the same as a conquered king is presented before those who have defeated him in battle. What a great picture of our great God, who, in spite of His people's confusion and His enemies' delusion, was victorious over both. And when the ark was finally returned to Israel, the Philistines had a new respect for the God of Israel, and so did the people of Israel.

It took twenty years of mourning their sin and stupidity and seeking to right themselves with Jehovah again, but finally Samuel, the fearless leader of all Israel by this time, told the people of God that it was time for them to put up or shut up. In advice that is applicable to followers in any era, Samuel told God's people how to reestablish the relationship that saves. God's people must rid themselves of anything that stands between them and God (whether it is other "gods" we have come to depend upon or a relationship, an activity, or a possession that distracts and detracts from the true God). God's true children must also commit themselves wholeheartedly to the God who can and will take care of all their needs (*believe* who He is and *know* that God is all we will ever need). And finally, God's people are called to serve Him faithfully—to worship Him only, to obey Him fully, to love Him completely, and to represent who He is to the rest of the world.

Samuel led a reform that swept the nation. During Samuel's tenure, God's hand was against the Philistines, Israel's territory was restored, and the people of God enjoyed a time of peace. Samuel continued throughout his life to be judge over all Israel, to be their priest, and to be God's prophet. He was everything they needed in a leader. As it turns out though, he wasn't everything they *wanted* . . .

AN APPALLING APPEAL

One day the elders of Israel got together and approached Samuel with some complaints and a petition. They told him that he was too old to be their leader, that his sons were too wicked to be their leaders, and that they had a real desire for something else. They laid before Samuel their request—which sounded much like a demand—that he appoint a king to lead Israel, to go before them, and to fight their battles.

Their request saddened Samuel because it sounded as if he was being spurned. But when he took it before God in prayer, the Lord told him that Israel wasn't rejecting him as their leader. They were renouncing God. Lord Jehovah, God Almighty himself, was the one who had visibly and unerringly led His people. (Remember the Red Sea, the cloud and fire, the Law!) He was the one who had gone before them. His name was the name people feared when they thought of Israel. His reputation upheld Israel's standing among the peoples of the world. He was the one who had fought their battles. (Remember Egypt, Jericho, and Canaan? Remember the Philistines?) What is it about our fleshly nature that demands a leader in the flesh? As much as Israel's rejection of God's kingship must have grieved Him, the *why* had to hurt God even more.

Israel was God's nation! It had been divinely established on Abraham with a promise. It had been divinely developed through Moses with the Law. The nation had been uniquely founded and celestially guided to serve God's holy purpose. They existed to bring God's precious Seed to the world. They were to glorify God *in* the world and clarify God's plan *for* the world. They were to be so different from the world around them that the world would come to them to find out why they were different.

Yet the people now wanted a king so they could be *like* the nations around them. God's chosen people didn't want to be special. They wanted to appear normal, not noticeably set apart from the people they wanted to impress. Who really wants to be God's "peculiar" people anyway? This is one of the things I agonize about regarding the church today. How much like the lost do we need to appear in order to appeal to the lost? Do we run the risk of not even looking like Christians in order to make Christianity palatable to the masses? Surely it is food for thought as we follow the modern method of building a better mousetrap in order to bring the unchurched into the church. Israel felt a real need not to stand out too much from the world around them, so they begged for a "better" leader than the one they had, or at least one more like everyone else's.

Finally fed up with their continuing vacillation and rejection of His leading, God destroyed them, right? No, He gave them what they wanted. Once again, on that day—and to this day as well—He allowed His people to *choose.* Then He would allow them to live with their choice. Remember, in our choices our hearts are revealed, and God instructed Samuel to tell the people where their choice would lead. So Samuel, speaking God's prophetic words, warned the people that anyone they allowed to rule them would one day own them, their possessions, and their offspring and would abuse his power over them. Then a day would follow when they would cry to God for relief from the king they had chosen, and in that day, God, their rejected king, would not answer their call. With God's warning ringing in their ears, the people cried out that they wanted a king anyway. And God responded with something like, "You asked for it. You got it!"

O SAUL, O ME, OH . . .

If Israel had remembered anything of their history, God's acquiescence should have caused an *uh-oh!* in their minds. But their hearts were so full of what they wanted that they couldn't think of anything else. So God chose Saul as their first king. Omniscient God, who knows all things in all times, knew how the human choice would turn out, but I'm convinced God chose Saul because he was the kind of king the people would have chosen for themselves. God's people had much to learn about the heart of God and about their own hearts as well. Therefore God gave them what they wanted: a man after their own heart.

Saul was tall and tan and young and handsome, and though he might not have swayed like a samba when he walked, when Saul passed, each Israelite he passed said, "Ahhhh . . . " Israel loved their new king. He would definitely have received the People's Choice Award. And he would become a king who would crave that acclaim from his people.

Saul stands as a monument to the axiom "Appearances are deceiving." He looked so great, and by the people's estimation, he was just what they needed in a king. He had a brief time as an effective ruler, but in the long run Saul would not build cities, organize the government, encourage art or literature, or practice or promote true religion. But he would lead Israel in victory against their enemies and give them military standing among their neighbors, those "everyone else" people who mattered so much to them. Israel looked tough while Saul was king. That was what they wanted: a *man's* man.

Throughout Saul's reign, Samuel kept urging him to be God's man. Instead, Saul wanted to *be* a man's man to impress the people, whose praise he craved (watch out!), yet he periodically attempted to *look like* God's man to impress Samuel, whose relationship with God he needed. Saul's pride and his need to look good to the people of Israel would be his downfall, because it would supersede his desire to look good for Samuel and God.

THAT SAUL YOU NEED TO KNOW

It started small, as most problems do. Saul won some battles and reveled in the praise it brought from the people. Then his son Jonathan won a battle, and Saul took credit for that as well. He began to trumpet his own greatness throughout the land. He began to imagine himself as the *ruler* of Israel. He made an executive decision to become the chief executive of Israel. First in pride, then in defiance, Saul chose to go against God's prophet and then against God himself.

One day when Samuel was late arriving to make an offering to God before a battle, Saul arrogantly decided to take Samuel's place as priest in order to stop his men from deserting the battlefield and to start God working in the battle. Saul was the king! He could do what he wanted. When Samuel arrived, he was scandalized by Saul's behavior, which was against God's law and Samuel's instructions. Only God's chosen priest was supposed to offer the sacrifice. On that day Samuel informed Saul that he had lost his exalted place in the nation of Israel. God, through the prophet, informed the king that his reign would in every way be coming to an end. By his disobedience to God, Saul would lose the greatest desire of his heart: greatness. Saul's family would be removed from the throne of Israel and be replaced by a man of God's own choosing, a man whose family, unlike Saul's, would occupy Israel's throne in perpetuity. Saul had been given every chance to keep God's commands and maintain his place in God's kingdom as God's king. Yet he had steadfastly refused to relinquish his heart to God's guidance, and therefore God would seek out a "man after his own heart" to be the new leader of His people.

The Saul nature lurks within us all. We have a hard time remembering what God wants when we get caught up in what we want.

One would think such an admonition from God would have smacked Saul back on the straight and narrow path, but, lest we forget, Saul was man's man. And lest we get too judgmental, we need to remember that the Saul nature lurks within us all.

We have a hard time remembering what God wants when we get caught up in what we want, which is often the same thing Saul wanted: the praise of others. Seemingly unaffected by Samuel's message from God regarding his fate and apparently ignorant of the fickleness of followers, Saul blithely continued about his kingly duties as he saw them, fighting battles for the hearts of the people of Israel.

And that leads us to the battle that Saul won while finally losing the war. It came as a result of orders Saul should have been thrilled to carry out: a chance to utterly destroy some ancient enemies—and, in doing so, to be God's tool. Saul was commanded by God to exact revenge for an old wrong, vengeance that God himself had promised centuries before. The Lord told Saul to absolutely wipe out the Amalekite people, who had waylaid the Israelites after their exit from Egypt. (Remember how God told Moses to write it down that He would deal with the Amalekites' treachery against His people?)

Saul, instead, made another executive decision: he decided to allow a small exception to God's command to utterly destroy everything. (By the way, God doesn't much care for "excepts" when He gives a holy edict.) Saul decided to spare the king and the best of the Amalekites' treasures to be used for the people, and these things "they were unwilling to destroy." It was probably that particular symptom of Saul's lack of regard for God's will that prompted Him to grieve that He had made Saul king. Saul was simply *unwilling to obey* God.

As a result of Saul's disregard and disobedience, God sent Samuel to deal with the unruly ruler. The king's excuse was that he gave in to the people's request because he was afraid of them. Obviously what he was afraid of was losing *their* regard instead of God's. His need for people's admiration and approval, more than any of his other character flaws, would cost Saul what he valued most. Samuel informed Saul that God had torn the kingdom from him and given it to one who was "better."

What You See Isn't Always What You Get

"Better" hardly begins to describe the man God chose to replace Saul. Very soon after He rejected Saul's leadership, the Lord set about choosing the king who would go down in the Bible as the standard for all kings who would follow.

One might think that the anointing of such a king would be the cause of much ceremony and that the coronation would be viewed by the masses. Instead, the event wasn't even an event: it was clandestine, witnessed by only a few bewildered relatives, and the celebrity wasn't even invited to the celebration!

Shortly after the prophet Samuel delivered the deathblow to Saul's hopes for immortality, God called Samuel to take his anointing horn and walk to the city of Bethlehem. At the home of a man named Jesse, God would introduce the prophet to the Lord's choice for king. It would become clear that not even Samuel truly understood God's heart in this matter, because the prophet was going to get a lesson in what really matters to God.

When Samuel arrived at Jesse's home and viewed his sons, he was impressed. The eldest looked very kingly to the old prophet, and Samuel assumed he might be gazing upon Israel's next king. Jesse's firstborn son was, like the current king, tall and tan and young and handsome and would most likely be viewed by the people as a splendid successor. I've always wondered how vigorous God's voice was in the old prophet's ear as He proclaimed they had been down this road before. "Do not consider his appearance or his height," God said to Samuel. "The LORD does not look at the things man looks at. Man looks at the outward appearance, but the LORD looks at the heart." God didn't want Samuel looking at the facade that only appears kingly; instead He wanted the prophet to know how *the Lord* views the makeup of a man. God assured Samuel that He knew exactly what He was looking for, and it had nothing to do with how anyone looked. And that meant Jesse's next good-looking son was not the one either. Nor was the next one, nor the next . . .

Seven sons of Jesse paraded before the prophet without being chosen by God as the king. The old prophet was confused and asked Jesse if he had any more sons. Belatedly Jesse remembered there was one more—the youngest and obviously the least memorable—"but he is tending the sheep." And there you have it. Israel's future king was out in the pasture, faithfully doing the job that would qualify him to lead God's people. He was being a shepherd.

So Jesse's youngest and least likely son was anointed as the future king of Israel. And what did he do after his anointing? He went back to the pasture and more shepherding. His heart for his father's sheep forecasted his heart for his Father's sheep. Psalm 78 states that God chose David *as* a shepherd to *be* a shepherd: "He . . . took him from the sheep pens; from tending the sheep . . . to be the shepherd of his people. . . . And David shepherded them with integrity of heart; with skillful hands he led them."

How many times during the next tumultuous decade or so of David's life do you suppose he wondered if he had just imagined that he had been anointed king? He was going to discover what most of God's great leaders discover: the call to lead God's people usually first requires them to follow Him through desolate territory in order to be fully prepared for the role. David would spend years serving a volatile and

The call to lead God's people usually first requires them to follow Him through desolate territory.

unstable Saul, years fleeing for his very life from the man whose love would turn to violent hatred, and years pouring out his heart in psalm song to God. But in all the years, through all the turmoil, in all the songs, David would prove why he was called.

SINGING IN THE REIGN

Sometime after the secret anointing, God's Holy Spirit took up residence in David and simultaneously departed from Saul. As the future king reveled in God's presence, the old king became tormented in His absence. No one seems certain what is meant by an evil spirit moving in to fill Saul's emptiness, but the result of God's retreat and the arrival of an evil replacement was that Saul became what we amateurs call "crazy." In desperation over the state of their king, Saul's servants dragged his future replacement into the palace to ease Saul's mood with the sound of music. Even though young David was already recognized as a man of valor, a warrior, a speaker of beautiful words, a fine-looking fellow, and one who had the Lord's presence, they primarily sought his skills as a musician to soothe the savage beast their king had turned into.

Apparently, and seemingly inappropriately for our holy God, the Almighty used an evil spirit to bring Saul and David together. But, remember, God's understanding of "good" and ours are frequently quite different. Obviously by God's design and for His purpose, David entered Saul's service, and both men gained something valuable from the association. Saul's malaise was temporarily relieved by the soothing sounds of David's harp and perhaps even by the faith-filled words of the psalms he sang over the desolate king. David was able to observe Saul and the activities in his palace and learn, as the future king, what makes a king. By observing Saul up close and personal, he also likely learned what doesn't make a good king. Saul took a great liking to David while he lived in the king's court, only belatedly realizing that he would soon take a pretty good beating because of him.

A REALLY BIG SHOW

Saul's beating began when the Israelite army was taking a beating at the hands of the Philistines. David, who apparently went back and forth from Saul's palace to the sheep pasture, depending on the king's state of mind, arrived at the Israelite encampment one day with food from Jesse for his older sons, who were serving in Israel's army. Almost as soon as David arrived at the scene, he was caught up in an event that would catapult him into the sight of all Israel. When David met Goliath, Israel met God's idea of a king.

Goliath was indeed an imposing figure and is described in great detail: a trained warrior from his youth, something like nine and a half feet tall, wearing upwards of 150 pounds of armor, carrying a nearly 40-pound spear, while having his shield carried by another man completely. Goliath had to have been a frightening figure.

When David arrived, Goliath had been taunting Israel for forty days, twice every day. Eighty times the heathen warrior had challenged the chosen people to send a warrior to fight him. There were no takers. The offer of riches, marriage into the royal household, and tax-free status for the entire family had inspired not one soldier to take a chance. And Israel's "biggest" soldier, the king described as a "head taller than any of the others," was apparently cowering in his tent. God's shepherd arrived at a battle that not one of God's soldiers wanted to fight. And when David heard Israel's silent response to Goliath's challenge, he considered their lack of words to be fighting words.

It turns out that the twelve spies who had spotted "giants" in Canaan when Israel first approached the Promised Land centuries before hadn't been exaggerating. Apparently some pretty big guys were still hanging around! And just as God's people had let the thought of those giants frighten them away the first time, they were afraid of this giant too. Isn't that how our own belief in God works

We can't see God for the giants that block our view. When all we see are our giants, we are refusing to see the God who has promised to defeat them for us.

sometimes? We can't see God for the giants that block our view. The giants we keep on fearing will keep on turning up. When all we see are our giants, we are refusing to see the God who has promised to defeat them for us.

That's what got David all stirred up: Israel's fear that the Philistines' giant was bigger than their God. David was indignant at Israel's refusal to believe in the power of their God. All that Israel saw was a giant. David saw an even bigger problem. He saw disgrace being brought on Israel and, even worse, on the Almighty God of Israel by a heathen warrior who could find no one with enough faith in God to fight.

Every day that Goliath challenged Israel's army and cursed the name of Israel's God without a response from His people was another day that both the Philistines and the Israelites began to suspect that the God of Israel might, in the face of a giant challenge, be impotent. If Israel had truly believed in God's power (oft demonstrated on their behalf), there should have been at least the glimmer of hope that He would assist any warrior faithful enough to accept Goliath's challenge. But every day, twice a day, Goliath had mocked Israel for coming out and assuming battle position while steadfastly refusing to engage in battle. He defied "the ranks of Israel" and challenged the "servants of Saul." And there we see the problem: the army of Israel now completely reflected the leadership of King Saul instead of King God. That was really bad news.

But there was some really good news. Goliath's jeering and Israel's silence reached the ears of the future king, a young man who had, with the acknowledged help of God, already defeated predators who had attacked the flocks he so diligently guarded. And the man who would one day guard God's flock decided at that moment to try his hand at defeating a giant. The shepherd boy volunteered to be a soldier. Upon later reflection, Saul might have second-guessed his own reluctance to fight, because after David's defeat of Goliath, David became the biggest sensation ever to hit Saul's kingdom, eclipsing Saul himself in a *giant* way.

David went into battle against Goliath with no armor, only a sling and stones and the name of the Lord on his lips, and he quickly dropped the Philistine behemoth and gained a gargantuan following in Israel.

WHAT GOES UP MUST COME DOWN

As soon as David dispatched Goliath, the Philistines fled in fear, galvanizing the army of Israel to act brave and pursue the pagans, plunder their camp, and ponder what had really happened in the dramatic victory they had just witnessed. Even Saul himself started wondering. He ordered his general to inquire whose son David was, and he sent for David so he could view him closely and discover just who he was. David arrived at Saul's tent holding the proof that he was someone to be reckoned with: the head of Goliath. And in rapid order, David captured the never-to-die loyalty of the king's own son, a high rank in the king's army, and the effusive praise of the king's minions. And there was the rub.

David's popularity among Saul's people was epoch-making. Israel began to sing his praises . . . literally. Some women greeted Saul one day with singing and dancing and a rhythm section with a fine beat that pounded into Saul's head, and not in a good way. The singers praised Saul's slaying of thousands, at which he must have preened, until they sang the chorus: that David had slain *tens* of thousands. Maybe it would have been okay if the song hadn't hit the Top Ten, but unfortunately for Saul, the song was a sensation. It was picked up by all the stations and rang out across the land, and soon the refrain "galled him." Most of my fifth graders don't know what that means, so I explain, as a former horse owner, about the spot that is rubbed on the back of a horse when a saddle doesn't fit correctly. The ill-fitting saddle rubs the same spot over and over until it becomes brutally painful to the touch, and the horse becomes either useless or very angry as a mount. That's what the women's refrain did to Saul. It rubbed him raw until he became very angry. And from that point on, the king began to keep a jealous eye on David.

And he began to try to get rid of David. The evil spirit that had previously inhabited Saul came back with a vengeance, and one day, overcome with fury, Saul tried to pin David to the wall with a spear. He feared David, because it was obvious that the Lord was with David, and the two of them in concert were an indomitable force. Saul had to get rid of his competition, but because of the people's love for David, he would have to choose a subtler method than harpooning him.

The king started by sending David off on missions impossible, hoping he would be killed. Unfortunately, David was always victorious, and his fame only grew. Trying a new approach, Saul offered his older daughter in marriage to David, hoping to humiliate him in Israel's eyes when he gave her to someone else instead. David turned down the offer, claiming he was unworthy of being in the king's family. Saul, undeterred, offered him yet another daughter, Michal, who already had a thing for David.

Saul reasoned that he could use her love to get David killed by someone other than himself. The payment for Michal's hand in marriage was a mere one hundred Philistine foreskins, which Saul was quite correct in assuming the Philistine men wouldn't turn over voluntarily. Any Philistine fighter who desperately wanted to hang on to his manhood, so to speak, should be motivated to kill the man who dared to take what really matters most to most males. Maybe David cared about Michal as much as she cared about him, or maybe it was the challenge to "buy" her with such panache that convinced David to pursue the private parts of a hundred men. Whatever inspired him, it was enough that he brought back two hundred Philistine foreskins while remaining unscathed by their previous owners. Obviously, neither subtlety nor subterfuge was working well for Saul.

Since the king's attempts at getting David killed by someone else merely increased David's popularity, Saul aimed his own spear at David again. He also ordered soldiers on more than one occasion to pursue and kill David. Each time, because the Lord was with him, David was saved from Saul's wrath. Finally, in desperation, Saul even tried to enlist the help of his son Jonathan, who was David's best friend and most loyal supporter. When Jonathan refused to help Saul kill David, Saul aimed his spear at his own son. It appears that deluded had gone to demented. Since his father had gone over the edge, Jonathan warned David that his best interest would be served by leaving the king's service and the kingdom. After taking an oath to always care for Jonathan and his descendants, David fled Israel, the nation that would someday be his domain, but not for a while and not for some miles.

JUST DESSERTS OR JUST DESERT?

When the shepherd went on the lam (okay, that isn't original, but it is irresistible), David entered a world familiar to most of God's great leaders: the wilderness. Abraham never got out of it once he got into it. Moses lived in and worked the area for eighty years. Elijah would soon become one of its associates. John the Baptist would preach in its environs. Jesus would be tempted there. Why do God's greatest need the wilderness? Because it's a lonely, hard place, a good place to be tested. And the only help God's child will find in the wilderness is God's help. Then when God's little one is alone and pressed and tested, he will discover that God's help is the only help he needs.

During David's tenure in God's wilderness, he endured the loss of his job, his wife, his friend, his prophet. He lost his place of honor. He nearly lost his mind. He eventually lost himself in the wilds of the desert land where he retreated. Yet he never lost sight of God. And that was why God never let him out from under His oversight. The man after God's own heart clung to the only thing he had left: God. During the wilderness years David poured out his heart to God in beautifully haunting psalms of woe and fear that called out for God's healing and protection, for God's salvation *in* the wilderness and eventually *from* the wilderness. David's life was in danger many times from many sides. Both foe and former friend tried to kill him, yet each time he was saved. At least twice he could have killed Saul, yet he refused to lift his hand against the Lord's anointed. He eventually gathered a small band of merry men who chose to follow him and would continue to support him when he assumed the throne of Israel. And gradually David's life turned around once again.

Saul's life on the other hand continued on its downward turn. Samuel died during David's wilderness years, and with his death, Saul lost his last link with God. He tried to call Samuel back from the dead through witchcraft, and when Samuel appeared by God's craft, the witch was as frightened as the king. Saul badly needed Samuel to once again intercede for him with God before a big battle, but instead Samuel informed the king that he would meet death in the coming skirmish. The next day Saul and his sons, including the wondrous Jonathan, died just as Samuel had predicted. An era had come to an end in Israel. *Israel's* king was dead. But *God's* king was now fully prepared to assume the throne in God's land.

14 THIS KING CAN SING, AND GOD IS HIS THING

KING DAVID

This is what the high and lofty One says—
he who lives forever, whose name is holy:
"I live in a high and holy place,
but also with him who is contrite and lowly in spirit,
to revive the spirit of the lowly
and to revive the heart of the contrite."

—ISAIAH 57:15

2 SAMUEL–1 KINGS 2

Do you imagine that David was the kind of guy who would have appeared on the cover of a celebrity magazine if they'd had such things back then? He apparently was a good-looking guy who attracted more than his share of female fans. If Saul had ever caught him during his flight through the wilderness, David probably would have had groupies waving banners in front of the jail, demanding his release, or even a few of those sadly psychotic marriage proposals that occur in such situations. In fact, his day in jail probably would have deserved a nightly recap on *E! Entertainment* news.

Or instead of being touted in entertainment magazines, David might have been featured on the front of *Sports Illustrated.* He appears to have been quite a jock as well, and great athletes certainly have just as devoted fans as other celebrities. David must have been quite a runner after evading Saul's army for years, and he might have qualified as a triathlete if you throw in rock slinging and savage-beast wrestling.

Then there's *Time* magazine, which surely would have named him as their man of the year, both for the support he had garnered among the down-and-out in the desert and the management skills that held his army of followers together. David looked like a good candidate to run a country: he had personal charisma, talent, and the backing of a devoted group of believers. He sounds like a winner to me. And even more important, he had the support of a Friend in really high places.

Life on the High Planes

David's time in the pasture, the palace, and the pits all combined to make him into a man whom God could trust to take His kingdom to heights of glory that would glorify God as king. Never lose sight of the fact that Israel was God's kingdom, and God had prodigiously prepared David to be a great ruler in His kingdom. For seven years after the death of Saul, David ruled only his own tribe, Judah, and battled Saul's remaining son and army for the rest of the land. When David finally ascended to the throne over all Israel, all Israel began the ascent toward that great nation God had promised to Abraham centuries before.

David reigned forty years, and during his rule Israel would become great—in God's eyes and the eyes of the rest of the world. One of the first things David did as ruler over Israel was to capture, fortify, and make Jerusalem the capital. It became the seat of government when he built his palace there and the seat of worship when he brought God's ark back there. It became Zion, "the City of David." During David's reign in the great city of Jerusalem, Israel became a world power. God's man was a military genius and a master of organization, and he ruled as a king should. He established a standing army and remained a warrior. He rid the land of its enemies and unified the tribes under a central government. He saw to the reorganization of Israel's worship and unified them under God's rule. "And he became more and more powerful, because the Lord God Almighty was with him." For the first time in its history as a nation, Israel was in control of the Promised Land, it was a great nation, and its name was great among the nations. Only one of the "big four" promises made to Abraham and his descendants was as yet unfulfilled: that Israel would bless all nations. And God was about to promise David that the remaining promise would also come to pass.

Despite all his accomplishments, David wanted to accomplish one thing for God. He wanted to build a house for Him. "After the king was settled in his palace and the LORD had given him rest from all his enemies around him, he said to Nathan the prophet, 'Here I am, living in a palace of cedar, while the ark of God remains in a tent.'" With almost embarrassing jubilance, David had honored God by bringing the ark of the covenant into Jerusalem, and now he wanted to build a permanent place for it to reside. But God had something else in mind, both for His house and for the house of David. Through the prophet Nathan, God told David that instead of him building a house for God, He would build a house for David, and the "house of David," his dynasty, would occupy the throne in God's nation as long as it existed. And through David's offspring would come a kingdom with a throne that would endure forever. Who would eventually come from the house of David? The King of kings, forever and ever, hallelujah, hallelujah! So, in a way, it was through David that God completed the promise He had given centuries before to Abraham: great land, great name, great nation, and the promise of great blessing to all nations through the One who would come and fulfill all promise.

Who eventually came from the house of David? The King of kings, forever and ever, hallelujah, hallelujah!

GETTING USED TO THE TOP OF THE ROOST

The scope of David's accomplishments as king over Israel was monumental and marvelous. He unified the people of his land, making them one nation under God. He destroyed all idol worship and was an active and a visible participant in the worship of the God who had put him on the throne. Every action David took acknowledged that it was indeed God's nation that he ruled. And the material blessings with which God blessed David reflected the value God placed on his spiritual commitment.

Few rulers have enjoyed more power and prestige than David did. He completely subdued his enemies by defeating them in battle, subjecting them to service, or convincing them that they would be better off as his allies. He opened Israel to commerce with the rest of the world, and Israel became a wealthy nation. He expanded Israel's territory by an order of magnitude. (According to my husband, the math major, that means you move the decimal point one space to the right. In this case Israel's territory went from approximately six thousand to sixty thousand square miles under David's rule.) And during the years he reigned, Israel became the most powerful nation of its day. Wouldn't it be great if his story ended with the greatness of Israel reflecting the greatness of their king and everyone holding hands and singing "Kumbaya" or standing in a circle and teaching the world to sing in perfect harmony? It never really ends like that though, does it?

David, for most of his life, had been hot. Now he was huge. And as so often happens, it may have been his undoing. The temptations that come with power and position are enormous. It happens to performers, politicians, and pastors alike. Sycophants and seducers come out of the woodwork when one achieves status, and it has to be tempting to believe that the flatterers are accurate. Different rules seem to apply to famous people and wealthy people and powerful people, and that, too, must begin to seem right. We don't know how much of that pertained to David, but we do know that in the midst of being one of the greatest rulers of all time, he made a few mistakes in ruling himself and his own family.

A BAA, BAA, BAD MOVE FOR THE SHEPHERD

I'm grateful my story is not one God feels compelled to share with the rest of the world. My life certainly could not stand the scrutiny. Most people's lives couldn't. Second Samuel 11 uses an enormous lens, like the ones on the cameras of the paparazzi, to give us a detailed picture of one of the most sordid acts ever recorded in the life of a godly man. Even people who are basically biblically illiterate know something about the episode. If they are asked to fill in the blank "David and ____," most will respond with "David and Goliath," followed closely by "David and Bathsheba." The story of David and Bathsheba is another one that takes careful telling to ten-year-olds, but I do tell it—delicately—because it teaches a lesson about David we can learn nowhere else. That glimpse into the dark corners of David's heart and the events that follow give us another reason why the Lord designated David as a man after His own heart.

David had been king for some time when he encountered Bathsheba. He had accomplished great things, written great psalms, and become recognized as a great man. He had also taken on a great deal of extra responsibility, including marriage to a great number of wives (and lack of marriage to numerous concubines) who had produced a great number of sons. By now David was middle-aged, and his life had assumed a kind of routine. Maybe that helps explain what happened. Maybe he was a little bored. After all, God had given him rest from all his enemies, and the nation of Israel was now running like the proverbial top, thanks to the organization David had put in place. He no longer had to fight; he no longer had to plan. He was on cruise control as a king. Or maybe he was just plain tired. He had been a fighter since his youth as a shepherd on constant watch over his flocks, and the kind of rest God had given him in his public life probably didn't translate very well to his private life in a household full of wives and children always jockeying for position. Whatever was

In quick order David entertained the temptation, followed up on the temptation, and then followed through on the temptation.

going on in the life of David when he got a glimpse of Bathsheba, we get a glimpse of what happens when even a man after God's own heart loses his way.

The story of David's fall begins by setting the stage. It was springtime in Israel, and according to the opening words, it was "the time when kings go off to war." Apparently in the spring, the winter rains are gone, the roads are dry enough to move an army, the larder is still filled with the autumn harvest, and food is available for an army on the move. And what do kings do when it is time to go to war? They go off to war! So what did the king of Israel do? He "sent" his army to war. His army won one battle and started another. And the leader of the army? He "remained in Jerusalem." That doesn't sound so bad. The army was winning without their king being with them, so what's the problem? The problem is that sometimes when we are not doing what we are supposed to be doing, we end up doing something we are not supposed to do.

So David was not in his rightful place at the right time and consequently ended up in the wrong place at the wrong time. He became a witness to something he was not supposed to see, and then he became a participant in something he was not supposed to do. Maybe (as some apologists for David suggest) Bathsheba shouldn't have been bathing on the roof where she was visible from David's palace, but while she might not have been circumspect in her choice of spas, she certainly did not cause David to sin and keep on sinning as he did. Scripture never casts the responsibility for what happened on Bathsheba, but David is another story.

What David saw from his palace rooftop that spring evening was a beautiful sight. Again, the Bible physically describes very few people, but Bathsheba is described as *very* beautiful. (That's a whopping description in biblical terms, considering that "lovely" was enough to make Jacob weak over Rachel.) The view from David's palace roof that night was enough to make him stop and linger in admiration. In quick order David *entertained* the temptation he encountered, *followed up* on the temptation by checking into who the woman was, and then, even after finding out she was the wife of one of his best soldiers and therefore definitely off-limits, he *followed through* on the temptation by sending men to bring her to him for a seriously sinful encounter. Then when he was done with his temptation, David allowed Bathsheba to return home, his lust assuaged, his boredom relieved—everything back as it should be. He might never have carried things any further if it hadn't been for one little side effect of his sin.

Most of us have given in to the kind of sin that swoops in and knocks us off our feet, so we may understand what happened to David that night on the roof. But how in the world can we explain what happened next? Sometime after the encounter in the palace, Bathsheba sent word to David that she had become pregnant as a result of their encounter. That's when it began to get really ugly. Sin is ugly enough on its own, but when we try to fix it on our own, it gets ugly indeed.

David first tried to repair things by *tricking* Bathsheba's husband into thinking the baby was his. The king pulled Uriah away from doing what he was supposed to be doing (fighting the king's battle) and sent him home to spend time with his beautifully tempting wife. But Uriah was too faithful to the king's army to give in to the tempting offer. The next night David tried to get Uriah drunk enough that he would give in to the temptation that had certainly been sufficient for David when he was sober. That plan didn't work either, and David found himself running out of options.

So he decided to get rid of his problem. David sent Uriah back to the army with a note to his commander to make sure that the faithful soldier would die in the next battle. David was very specific to his commander about how Uriah's death should take place, thus involving another man in murder. Lust, adultery, deceit, murder, involving others in ungodly acts—sin never seems to shrink, but it surely can grow! It can also surely deceive. Assuming he had gotten away with his sins or deciding that because he was the king, he could brazen his way through it all, David absolved his commander of his participation, "mourned" the death of a good man, and took Bathsheba to be his wife (another one). And the chapter on David and Bathsheba ends with this sobering statement: "But the thing David had done displeased the LORD."

IT'S NOT ALWAYS BEST TO BE "THE MAN"

Do you think "displeased" is another one of those biblical understatements? I think it might have been. Because sometime after David's sin and cover-up, after David had relaxed into his sin and was convinced that everything was all right, God sent the prophet Nathan with a parable for David. The parable told of a wealthy man who owned flocks of sheep yet slaughtered the much-loved and only lamb of his poor neighbor in order to feed an important guest. David was so incensed that he declared the villain deserved to die. Upon that declaration, Nathan spoke God's message to David: "You are the man!"

Could anything more deeply pierce David's heart than knowing the Lord he loved so much knew what a sinner he was? (I think sometimes when we have fooled others, and ourselves, we tend to believe we've fooled God as well.) The words God spoke through His prophet reflected His pain at David's sin: "I anointed you king over Israel, and I delivered you from the hand of Saul. I gave your master's house to you, and your master's wives into your arms. I gave you the house of Israel and Judah. *And if all this had been too little, I would have given you even more.*" David was absolutely smitten with remorse upon hearing the Lord's words. His response, "I have sinned against the LORD," reflected his contrition and his recognition of where he stood with God. And by his response, David proved just why God knew that David's heart was indeed His.

Sometimes when we have fooled others, we tend to believe we've fooled God as well.

In heartrending poetry, David poured himself out in Psalm 51. Having sinned against his holy God, he knew the only place to turn was to the holy God who was also his loving Lord. David was like a small child who, chastened and heartbroken by his mother's punishment, grabs the only comfort he can find: his mother. When the sobbing child wraps his arms around his mother and buries his face in her chest, he is expressing every confidence that she still loves him. And when she wraps her arms around him, she is assuring him that she does. That's the picture we get in this beautiful psalm of confession, contrition, and concession. David trusts God to be God: unfaltering Judge, unfailing Love. He absolutely throws himself at the mercy of the God he trusts, who has never let him down. The psalmist admits the sin was his alone, blaming no one else and making no excuse for his trespass against God's holy commandments. He vows to align himself once more with God's way and pledges to teach others about God's will. And then, in all things a man after God's heart, the singer of God's songs acknowledges one other thing about his God. Holy God, in making things right again, has the right to punish David.

And He did.

Like the man in Nathan's parable, David deserved to die for his terrible sin. Instead, he would suffer terrible consequences. Even forgiven sin has consequences. And rest assured in this: God did forgive David and never once recanted the title He had bestowed upon him as a man after His own heart. When God spoke of David's offspring, He probably spoke of David as well, saying, "When he does wrong, I will punish him with the rod of men, with floggings inflicted by men. But my love will never be taken away from him." David would indeed be punished, and in pretty short order he found out that the punishment would, as they say, fit the crime. Since David had destroyed the household of Uriah by the sword, the sword of treachery and death would destroy his own house as well. "Calamity" would fall upon the household of the king. His child with Bathsheba would be a casualty of his sinful and selfish encounter, as the child, too, would die. God also informed David that just as he had taken the wife of someone close to him, someone close to David would take his wives and lie with them in broad daylight for all to see. There were to be some pretty bad consequences—in recognition that it had been some pretty bad sinning.

My Three (and Twenty!) Sons

David had at least eight wives and at least twenty sons. It seems he was a pretty busy man in the off season when he wasn't occupied with "kinging," and it would be his nonkingly behavior that would be used against him. Like a number of good men in the Old Testament (including Eli and Samuel, both of whom David should have been aware of as recent examples), David was a very good man who turned out not to be a very good father. That happens a lot to people in important positions, doesn't it? They get so caught up in a career or position or solving other people's problems or even leading other people's children to the Lord that their own problems go unsolved, their own family gets lost, and they soon find out that all their success in one area is not enough to prevent failure in another. As a ruler for God's nation, King David was unequaled. In fact he would become the measuring stick for all the kings after him. Yet the ruler's home would be ripped asunder, and his own family would reveal just how little respect they had for him. With these two extremes measuring David's forty years as king over God's kingdom, his reign would stumble to an end.

Although Israel's enemies on the outside had been vanquished by David's strength, the interior of the nation would be splintered because of his weakness. His sons fought against each other and against him. The son born from his sin with Bathsheba died. One of his older sons raped his half sister and was killed by her brother. His favorite son slept with ten of his concubines on the rooftop so that all Israel could see David's humiliation. At least two of his sons tried to steal the throne from him, and one of them was that favorite son whom David continually failed to discipline and refused to let anyone else discipline. It does seem fitting that his favorite, Absalom, was the one who may have given him the most problems and definitely caused him the most grief. (It also seems fitting that the extremely spoiled and very vain Absalom would die from a "bad hair day." I always knew it could seriously damage your psyche, but kill you? Wow!) Nathan's prophecy of sword and calamity within the family of David didn't take long to be fulfilled, and David lived out his final days far from the glory days of his youth.

ONE, TWO, THREE, SOLOMON'S AFTER ME

When David was an old man and in failing health, his son Adonijah decided to become the next king of Israel. David, and more importantly God, determined that the next king of Israel should be a different son, the son of David and (trumpets, please) Bathsheba! I do love the way the Lord works. God would add Bathsheba to the genealogy of Jesus Christ. She joins four other women in a long list of men named as ancestors of the Christ in the first chapter of Matthew. Apart from Mary, it's a perplexing list. There's Tamar, who dressed as a prostitute in order to sleep with her father-in-law, Judah. There's Rahab, the woman of ill repute from the city of Jericho. There's Ruth, who was a foreigner, and then there's Bathsheba, the adulteress. (She is named only as "had been Uriah's wife," so isn't that interesting!)

If we weren't primarily looking at the character of our holy God in this book, we might not grasp why such things happen in the Holy Book. I believe that these women, each of whom had a reason she "should not" have been listed in the lineage of our Lord, are there to demonstrate more about God's character than their own. He wants us to know that He can *redeem* the lost, He can *cleanse* the impure, He can *include* the outsider, and He can *make right* what seems very wrong to those of us who look only on the outward appearance.

> *He wants us to know that He can redeem the lost, cleanse the impure, include the outsider, and make right what seems very wrong to those of us who look only on the outward appearance.*

Is it surprising that God always claimed David as "His," especially when we realize that David was shockingly like us instead of like God? Did you know that David never quit sinning? In fact he kept on making mistakes right till the bitter end. But each time he made the kind of errors that humans make, he knew where to go. David always went right back to God, who so loved this very *human* being. If David does nothing else for me, he gives me hope that the God who loved David and listed sinners in the lineage of His one and only Son can, surprisingly, love someone like me as well.

Before David died, he passed on words of wisdom to the future king of Israel. He told him to be strong, to observe what the Lord requires, to walk in God's ways, to keep God's decrees, and to watch how he lived before God. If his son did all that, David assured him that he would prosper in all he would do and God would keep His promise to bless the family of David in perpetuity.

They were wise words from the godly king. And Solomon, chosen as David's successor, seemed to be a wise choice as well

15 A KING WITH SOME BLING, AND LOOK WHAT *THAT* BRINGS!

KING SOLOMON

You, my son Solomon, acknowledge the God of your father,
and serve him with wholehearted devotion and with a willing mind,
for the LORD searches every heart and
understands every motive behind the thoughts.
If you seek him, he will be found by you;
but if you forsake him, he will reject you forever.

—1 CHRONICLES 28:9

1 KINGS 3–11; 2 CHRONICLES 1–9

I have only one son, so Mark is both my best and my worst son. My daughter claims she is "from Mars," as in the men being from Mars and women being from Venus scenario (and she is), but she still isn't a son. That leaves me with only one, who is, by the process of elimination, my best son. (Kasey, while conceding she isn't my best son, would not be so conciliatory if I had to choose my best child. In fact, she has repeatedly and jubilantly expressed her approval of my mothering skills by pointing out what a good job I did raising the spectacular human she has become.) If I did have more than one son, and only one of them could be the heir apparent of all the good titles and good things I could pass along, I'm sure I would have a really hard time picking one over the other. I wonder if David, on his own, would have picked Solomon from all his sons to succeed him as king. We can't be sure which son David would have chosen, but we can believe that God knew exactly who to choose in order to accomplish what He needed His kingdom to accomplish. The choice of Solomon and the results of his reign will once again prove that God moves in mysterious ways His "do you ever wonders" to perform.

By what seemed right to most people maybe Solomon shouldn't have been the next king of Israel. As many sons as David had, surely some were older than Solomon and may, by right, have considered themselves heir to the throne. However, it was God who decided on Solomon, and He, by His very nature, is right in all things. And when Solomon chose to receive wisdom from God in order to rule His kingdom well, everything seemed right on. Wouldn't it be nice if just once things worked out as they "should"?

SING A SONG OF SOLOMON

A casual observer of the life of Solomon would rightfully be very impressed with the man and the king. King Solomon was a prolific writer of proverbs (three thousand), songs (one thousand), books of the Bible (three), and numerous teachings on botany and zoology. David's son ruled in peace during the golden age of Israel, most of the peace and much of the gold being gifts from his father's days of frequent and bloody war, new and strong alliances with former enemies, and divine blessings from above. Solomon was wealthy in the extreme and wise beyond parallel. Seekers came to hear his wisdom. Tourists came to view the edifices he had built. During Solomon's reign, Israel was at its peak of power and prestige. Israel was a great nation. Jerusalem was famous, the most splendid city of its day, and its temple was the most magnificent building the world had yet seen. What a time! What a place! What a king!

God heaped blessings on Solomon. He appeared to Solomon one night in a dream and told him that he could ask for whatever he wanted. Solomon, being really wise for a young man, sought a discerning heart in order to govern God's people and to distinguish between right and wrong. Delighted by Solomon's choice, God promised that He would also give him what he did not ask for. He would give him long life, riches, and honor. God would bless Solomon so much that "there will never have been anyone like [him], nor will there ever be." And to this day, he's considered the wisest man who ever lived and would certainly make it into the top tier of the wealthiest. With all that, how could anything go wrong?

A Song Slightly Off-Key

Before Solomon even had his first encounter with God, there are little clues to approaching problems in his kingdom and in his character. One of the very first things he did as king, before his wise alliance with God, was to make an alliance with the pharaoh of Egypt. As a seal on the deal, Solomon married the pharaoh's daughter and brought her to Jerusalem "until he finished building his palace and the temple of the LORD, and the wall around Jerusalem." God had chosen David's son to build the temple that David had so wanted to build, but before he built what he was meant to build, Solomon built an alliance with a nation that God had repeatedly urged His people to avoid. And the new king began to establish relationships that would one day play a large part in dismantling his nation.

In the same paragraph where we're told of Solomon's accord with Egypt, there are hints of discord in his own country: "the people, however, were still sacrificing at the high places." Is that a problem? There's not a temple yet. However, God had always been specific with the Israelites about how and where He wanted to be worshiped, and it was always to be a place of His choosing, not theirs. We're going to see that His choice was never the high places that the people chose over and over when left to their own devices. Which brings us to why God chooses the way and the place for His people to worship: people who want to choose how and where they worship frequently become people who start changing what or who they worship! Anytime people institute their own methods of worship, there's the danger that they will deviate from worship of the Lord God.

Where was Israel's godly leader, the builder of their future worship center, while the Israelites were beginning to modify their worship? First Kings 3:3 tells us where he was. When I have one of my fifth graders read this verse, I tell everyone to listen for one of those special words that periodically crop up in Scripture. So we read the verse: "Solomon showed his love for the LORD by walking according to

> *Anytime people institute their own methods of worship, there's the danger that they will deviate from worship of the Lord God.*

the statutes of his father David, except that he offered sacrifices and burned incense on the high places." The fifth graders always see it. The word just jumps off the page: "except." In Solomon's case, it was a big exception. Here's the new king of God's kingdom, and he's following in the steps and following the advice of his godly father, *except* not exactly. He worshiped the Lord, *except* not like the Lord wanted to be worshiped. It's a pretty big exception, all right, but it's not the only one. Solomon followed God, *except* he married a pagan to secure a treaty with a nation he was supposed to avoid. He was the wisest man who ever lived, *except* he wasn't very bright in some areas of his life. The third king of Israel was a very good king, *except* he would, by all the exceptions he made in his living, his worshiping, and his ruling, leave the nation of Israel on the brink of ruin when he died.

THE ROAD TO YOU-KNOW-WHERE IS PAVED WITH YOU-KNOW-WHAT

How can it all go so wrong so fast? Because it isn't fast. It's gradual; it's imperceptible; it's unintentional. It happens when we're not paying attention to what really matters and we're caught up in the incidentals of our lives. It creeps up on us while we're running full speed ahead toward our own accomplishments, our own accolades, our own accumulations. We don't even recognize it for what it is. We don't realize it holds such appeal for us. And when all is said and done, we are destroyed without ever realizing we were in danger. It can happen to any of us. It happened to wise Solomon.

Solomon had the *desire* to be a good king. That's obvious by his request for wisdom to govern God's people. He also was given all the *tools* he would need to be a really great king. Likewise, he had the *instruction manual* for being the kind of king God wanted—both in the pattern of his father and in the Law God had given to Moses. He *thought* he was doing a good job, I imagine. Everyone around him probably told him he was a good king. He *appeared* to be doing well if judged by the world's standards. People came from across the world to witness Solomon's accomplishments. The queen of Sheba traveled a thousand miles (from what is now Yemen) just so she could see for herself what he had done and hear for herself what he had to say. By every standard we can think of, Solomon excelled. In some areas he even exceeded the wonderful David. So what happened?

He didn't *intend* to go wrong. But he didn't *intend* to go right.

I think somewhere along the way Solomon got caught up in living like a king. How easy would that be for any of us to do? (How easy is it for us when we're *not* kings?) I don't know that Solomon intentionally broke the commandments for being a king. He probably just lost some of the nuances. He probably neglected to care about all the details (who needs this "legalistic" stuff anyway?) while he was caught up in the dailiness

He didn't intend to go wrong. But he didn't intend to go right.

of kingly living. However, one of the laws for the king was to write for himself a copy of the Law on a scroll, which he was to keep with him at all times so he could read God's Law and follow His decrees. Solomon might have saved himself, and Israel, a lot of heartache if he had simply followed that one law. I understand, and thus forgive, Solomon's shortcomings because of my own nature of being a *wanting* (lacking a necessary quality) and a *"wanting"* (desiring things) human being. But the truth is that Solomon, like all of us, made a pretty big mess of things when he lacked the right stuff and loved the wrong stuff.

A KING'S RANSOM

For an interesting and, frankly, quite frightening exercise, place Deuteronomy 17:14–20 (the law for Israel's king) side by side with 1 Kings 10:26–11:3 (the list of how Solomon shattered the law for Israel's king). It almost looks as though Solomon read the law and decided to flagrantly obliterate nearly every one of the decrees. Deuteronomy states that the king must not acquire great numbers of horses for himself, nor should he make the people return to the forbidden land of Egypt in order to get the horses. Yet 1 Kings proclaims that Solomon collected twelve thousand horses and fourteen hundred chariots, and he imported them from—Egypt! Deuteronomy urges the king not to accumulate large amounts of silver and gold. First Kings declares that the weight of Solomon's gold was twenty-five *tons* a year and that he made silver "as common in Jerusalem as stones." There are two "thou shalt not" laws that Solomon broke to smithereens.

But where he really went haywire was in the third law: "the king . . . must not take many wives, or his heart will be led astray." We read in 1 Kings that Solomon loved "many" women. What is "many"? Well, there were many varieties. Besides Pharaoh's daughter, he loved women who were Moabites, Ammonites, Edomites, Sidonians, and Hittites—all forbidden by God and each apt to lead Solomon away from God. "Many" also meant volume. He had seven hundred wives and three hundred concubines! That is *way* too many! If we thought Jacob was busy with four women and David had problems with twenty, imagine how overworked and plagued with problems Solomon was!

As for the accumulation of gold and silver by King Solomon, a lot of it was required for his building projects. The temple took seven years at the cost of $600 million in BC money, and at today's prices it would cost more than $40 billion. (That's *billion* with a *b*.) Solomon's palace took thirteen years to build and was pretty fine itself. The cost of building the kind of edifices that drew tourists to Israel went a long way toward destroying the nation. But then, so would the energy and devotion that Solomon spent on his women.

It's too bad Solomon couldn't have been a love 'em and leave 'em kind of guy. Being acquainted with a thousand women would have been bad enough for most men. But unfortunately Solomon loved his women. In fact, he "held fast to them in love." And *that* would be his undoing. Solomon loved his women so much that he built homes for them, and he built temples to their various gods so they could worship as they wanted. And in 1 Kings 11:4 we read the tragic words: "His wives turned his heart after other gods, and his heart was not fully devoted to the LORD his God." A no-hearted king hadn't been much good at building anything. A wholehearted king had built a great kingdom on God. Now a halfhearted king, who built a great building, would bring about the destruction of all that had been built.

DIVIDED LOYALTIES

What happens when the ruler of God's kingdom is not fully devoted to God? He can continue to try to rule by his wealth, his fame, his position, or his smarts. He can try. Yet when Solomon died, the world's wealthiest, most powerful nation of its time was near financial ruin and spiritual bankruptcy. Solomon was never a warrior, but he laid the powder that would blow his nation apart.

Solomon's extravagant lifestyle and the distraction of a thousand women cost Israel dearly. The king raised the people's taxes to painful levels. He pressed people into his service. Maybe the people of Israel recalled the Lord's warnings against wanting a king who would someday take the very best of their money, their time, their children, and all their resources; a king who would force them to work for him; a king who would in every way own them. But Solomon didn't seem satisfied with just taking their money and their time. He took away the foundation of what had made Israel great in the first place: he took Israel away from God.

Solomon allowed his wives to lead him toward idolatry. He "followed" Ashtoreth, the goddess of the Sidonians, and Molech, the terrible god of the Ammonites. He built places for the worship of Chemosh, the abhorrent god of Moab, and also for Molech. These were the vile, vain gods that Israel's holy God had ordered His people to remove from the Promised Land when they first entered. These pagan gods had been purged from the land, removed by the bloodshed of faithful men under the direction of God Almighty. Solomon brought them back.

> *He took away the foundation of what had made Israel great in the first place: he took Israel away from God.*

The Lord was not displeased with Solomon. He was *angry*. Much as He had told King Saul decades before, God told Solomon that He was going to "certainly" tear the kingdom away from him and give it to someone else. And He would. With the inward failure of an outwardly successful king, the united kingdom of Israel would come to an end.

But "for the sake of David," God would preserve the tribe of Judah for David's descendants who had important things yet to accomplish for the kingdom of God.

16 And Away We Go!

The Northern Kingdom

These people have stubborn and rebellious hearts;
they have turned aside and gone away.

—Jeremiah 5:23

1 Kings 12–2 Kings; 2 Chronicles 10–36

Samuel F. B. Morse, marveling at his new telegraphic contraption, sent as his first message "What hath God wrought?" It is certainly a question that could be asked in many circumstances, and it was probably a question the Israelites would like to have had answered as the magnificent reign of King Solomon came to its inglorious end. For a man who had started out with everything necessary to be a great king and to grow a great kingdom, Solomon had left his kingdom in a pretty bad state of affairs.

Maybe that was the problem. *Solomon's* kingdom had failed. Israel had begun its upward trajectory under the leadership of his father, David, who had completely recognized that Israel was, in all aspects, *God's kingdom*. But Solomon had shown signs all along that he was not of the same mind (nor especially of the same *heart*) as his father. For instance, Solomon spent seven years constructing God's temple and thirteen years building his own palace. Okay, maybe that's unfair. Maybe God's house was more important to finish and therefore took precedence over the building of his own home. I'd like, for Solomon's sake, to believe that was the case. But if God was preeminent in

Solomon's great mind, why didn't he worship in the temple instead of in the high places he seemed to prefer, and why didn't he follow God instead of worshiping pagan

One of Solomon's big problems was that he tried to span two worlds.

gods? And why did the temple built for Jehovah God become known across the world (and to this day) as Solomon's Temple? It seems that Solomon put a lot of himself into building Israel into the grand nation it became during his reign. And when it all came tumbling down, Solomon had only to look in his mirror to find the cause. Israel could blame God if they chose, but it had been at their instigation that any man had been placed as king over them, and the same king whose fame they gloried in would have to take the blame for what happened next. As would they.

One of Solomon's big problems was that he tried to span two worlds. He wanted to be an Israelite who loved foreigners. He wanted to build a temple for Jehovah God and altars for his wives' gods. He wanted to rule wisely, but he himself was ruled by foolish desires. Jesus assured His listeners that "no one can serve two masters," and any of us who have tried know that only one master will have mastery over us. Jesus assured His listeners that they would love one master and hate the other. In Solomon's case, the mistresses had the mastery over him, and his love for them led him to "hate" God's call to love only Him. It also led to the destruction of the nation of Israel.

An Unwise Reprise

The Lord spoke to Solomon toward the end of his reign. Unlike the beginning of his rule, when all things were possible and Solomon intended to rule well, God didn't ask Solomon what He could do for him. This time God *told* Solomon what He was going to do *about* him. Because of Solomon's idolatry and love for his wives over God, most of the kingdom was going to be taken away from his descendants. But for the sake of David and Jerusalem, God would honor the covenant He had made to keep the royal family of David on the throne in Jerusalem. But only in Jerusalem would the family reign. Solomon's kingdom was going to become just as divided as his heart had been.

Upon Solomon's death, his son Rehoboam was named king over all Israel. According to God's declaration and because Rehoboam obviously didn't inherit his father's wisdom, it wouldn't last long. One of Solomon's former servants, Jeroboam, received the prophetic message that he would rule ten of the twelve tribes, and he chose to accept the job, but first he gave Rehoboam the opportunity to be in control of both him and his ten tribes. I think Jeroboam might have known that Rehoboam hadn't inherited the smart gene, or surely he wouldn't have offered to serve Rehoboam. Nothing else about Jeroboam indicates that he was either subservient or interested in doing what was right.

Almost immediately Rehoboam set about proving he wasn't very wise. When Jeroboam offered to serve Rehoboam if he would lighten the tax burden that Solomon had imposed to support his ways and his wives, Rehoboam sought two opinions on what he should do. He first asked the older men who had served under Solomon if he should ease the burden on the people. The elders suggested that if Rehoboam served his people, they would gladly serve him. Not caring all that much for their suggestion of *his* service, Rehoboam inquired of his peers (those who *served him*) what he should do. The young and restless (and foolish) ones recommended that Rehoboam rule his people in such a way that they would scream for the good old days when Solomon's lifestyle had sucked them dry of all their resources. Rehoboam thought that sounded like a really good idea. (Have you ever noticed that the people whose advice you consider wise are the people who think exactly like you?)

Rehoboam thought he and his friends were really smart and would rule over everyone and everything. It turns out, though, that God ruled over all after all. In fact, we're told that the whole thing was "from the LORD" and fulfilled all that had been told to Jeroboam and to Solomon. And just to make sure Rehoboam knew where everyone stood, he, too, was told directly that it was the Lord's "doing." God's words to Solomon were fulfilled when Jeroboam took his ten tribes and seceded from the union. After 120 years as a great nation under God, the one became two, and the two became trouble.

IF AT FIRST YOU DON'T SECEDE

Jeroboam took his ten tribes and left David's tribe. In every way that it is possible to leave, they left.

Jeroboam was from the tribe of Ephraim, making him a descendant of Joseph's youngest son, who was blessed by Jacob over his own older brother and over most of Joseph's brothers as well. Jacob's continuing favoritism toward Joseph had driven a wedge between the brothers that Jeroboam's ascension to the throne could only have exacerbated. Now the two nations were ruled by the descendants of Ephraim (Joseph's son) and Judah (Joseph's brother who had received the "other" extra blessing). Maybe the remnant of hard feelings led Jeroboam to lead his tribe and the nine who followed them as far from their relatives as they could go, philosophically speaking anyway.

The twelve tribes remained close in borders only. The northern ten tribes took the name "Israel" (Jacob's name change) and were also periodically referred to as "Ephraim." The two southern tribes took the name of their largest tribe, "Judah," and incorporated the little tribe of Benjamin as well. Jeroboam didn't waste time in ensuring that the difference between Israel and Judah was not in name only.

Don't Have a Cow!

Immediately upon establishing a separate country, Jeroboam made sure his people would have no reason to return to Judah. If worshipers had to return to Jerusalem two or three times a year for religious feasts or festivals—as was required by law—there was a distinct possibility that loyalty to Jehovah might eventually overpower loyalty to Jeroboam. So the first thing the new king did was set up two new worship sites within his territory's boundaries, one easily reached from the north, the other easily reached from the south. Jeroboam began, among other things, a trend that continues today of making religion "convenient" for worshipers. Bethel, the southern site for worship, was only ten miles north of Jerusalem and was on the main road to the holy city. If the people started for Jerusalem to worship, they could choose an alternate, more accessible option instead.

In addition to giving his people a substitute for Jerusalem, Jeroboam gave them a substitute for Jehovah God. One of his first official acts as king was to introduce calf worship into Israel. The calf symbolized fertility and strength and was used in several of the Canaanite religions. But to me it always speaks of Egypt, and God had frequently urged His people never to return to Egypt. Yet for centuries after the four hundred years of captivity in Egypt, something about that nation, its plenty, and its gods continued to appeal to God's people. It was calf worship the people embraced at the foot of Mount Sinai when God was obscured behind the cloud and the lightning.

And it was calf worship that the people would embrace when their king decided to obscure once more their view of God. But Jeroboam wasn't satisfied with just *supplementing* the worship of Jehovah. He wanted to *supplant* the worship of the Holy One of Israel. He proclaimed to the people, "Here are your gods, O Israel, who brought you up out of Egypt." If you can change people's perspective of their past, you can change their present as well. It happens today in psychology when false memories are "recovered," yet they become real, and the past begins to rule the present. To pervert the Israelites' worship, Jeroboam perverted their history. The people began to believe that the golden calf was their real god and maybe always had been. Who needed Jerusalem anymore? Who needed Jehovah?

Speaking of needs, what needs to happen in order to have worship of the one true God evolve into something else entirely? Do we need any more than the Israelites did?

If you can change people's perspective of their past, you can change their present as well.

On my recent trip to Israel, our group traveled to the location of the old tribe of Dan, the northernmost territory during the time of the divided kingdom and the other site Jeroboam set up as an alternative for worship. We climbed to the high places through beautiful vegetation, with streams bubbling up from the ground all around. It was some of the most stunning scenery we saw during the entire trip (and it looked like a very nice setting for worship). On top of the hill, sitting in an excavated pagan altar, we had a devotional led by maybe the finest teacher of God's Word I've ever heard and a historical perspective presented by one of our gifted Israeli guides. Both men talked about how easily true worship can be perverted with just a few twists. According to the experts who research such things, the pagan altar site where we sat probably replicated in size and shape the temple in Jerusalem during Solomon's time. It was a place the worshipers of the day would be familiar with since Solomon's Temple had been dedicated only a couple of decades before the secession. If any of the worshipers were concerned about not going back to Jerusalem or not doing things exactly as they had in Jerusalem, they had only to observe that their new worship site appeared to be very similar to the old one, so maybe their worship wouldn't be that far off either. Just a little twist in form, just a small variation in style, just an innovative leader with exciting plans for improvement, just a new idea to correct old (fashioned) ways. . . .

Oh, yeah, and just a little change in gods as well. How many twists does it take to move people from thinking their worship is all right to believing it's more right? How many twists does it take to change our concept of who God is? How many twists until loving the God we worship is replaced by loving our worship?

Jeroboam did a masterful job of leading the people to do his will instead of God's, to follow his ways instead of God's, to believe in him instead of God. Do you know what phrase is used over and over when he is mentioned in Scripture? He is called Jeroboam, son of Nebat, who "caused Israel to sin." That is a lot of clout. The first king in the new kingdom of Israel *established* idol worship and even *presided* over some of the worship proceedings. He *instituted* new festivals and feasts, and he *allowed* anyone who wished to become a priest.

Finally a prophet of God gave the king a message from God: "You have done more evil than all who lived before you." Ahijah, who had formerly told Jeroboam he would be given the ten tribes, now told how God would remove everything from him. He told Jeroboam about the tribulation that would fall on his family because he had turned his back on God and carried his people far away from the Lord, who had raised him up. It was a gruesome forecast, involving fire, dogs, and flesh-eating birds, but for a man who made God's people sin, it was just.

Wouldn't it have been great if Jeroboam had changed his ways and altered Israel's direction in order to avoid such a hideous judgment? But I guess he was too far gone. He was so far away from God and had taken God's people so far with him that none of them could see, or hear, anything about God anymore. Jeroboam ruled in the northern kingdom of Israel for just over twenty years, but in those two decades he did irreparable damage that took a nation toward destruction. And the kings who followed him, followed his example.

AND NOW, FOLLOWING THIS . . .

Halley's Bible Handbook describes Israel's kings with words like "bad," "very bad," and "the worst." Revolutions and bloodshed occurred on a grand scale as one evil king followed another. Most of the kings who succeeded Jeroboam are described as "walking in the ways of Jeroboam and his sin." That's quite a testimony to Jeroboam's wickedness. One of the worst kings in the northern kingdom—the nefarious Ahab—was described this way: "He not only considered it trivial to commit the sins of Jeroboam son of Nebat, but he also married Jezebel [even more abhorrent than Ahab himself] daughter of Ethbaal king of the Sidonians, and began to serve Baal and worship him . . . and did more to provoke the LORD . . . to anger than did all the kings of Israel before him." The kings of Israel progressed from arrogant toward God to rebellious against God-worship to absolutely apostate in God's eyes. They added more and more gods to their worship, and their worship became more and more debauched. This was not a drifting away from God, as had previously happened in Israel's history. This was a willful plunge into depravity, and with few exceptions, the people of God willingly followed their leaders down the path to devastation.

Although leaders who precede and then persuade followers into ruin must bear the lion's share of the blame, those who follow meekly like lambs are not without responsibility for their own demise. We all get to choose whom we follow and how far and how willingly.

WHAT DOES IT PROPHET?

The exceptions to the people who sheepishly followed the kings of the north were quite exceptional. In fact, they were downright "different," if you want to know the truth. These men came to the people of God from out of the blue usually, often from the wilderness, once from a fish's belly. They were the prophets who spoke God's words in repeated attempts to call the people back to the dominion and protection they had enjoyed under His rule. The Lord God of Israel wanted His people to return to Him and His way.

In thunderous displays of God's power, the prophet Elijah revealed the Almighty's superior strength over the gods Israel had chosen to replace Him. In tender miracles of healing, the prophet Elisha demonstrated the merciful love God still had for His children. Jonah's reluctant missionary trek to Nineveh (capital of the wicked and powerful Assyrian Empire) and his equally reluctant success among them exhibited that God could forgive anyone, even His enemies. But of all the prophets the Lord Jehovah sent to the people of Israel, none expresses the *heart* of God more than Hosea.

The book of Hosea points out how Israel had failed to keep the covenant they had made with God on Mount Sinai, how they had refused to love God and even refused to acknowledge Him as God, how their leaders had rejected God and had preferred idols. The message was that the people of God had failed in the "marriage" that had occurred at Sinai. They had in fact prostituted themselves with other gods, repeatedly choosing perverted love and the pretense of love that is represented by prostitution. To demonstrate how God felt toward His apostate children, He commanded the prophet Hosea to love a prostitute who would refuse to love him back and would refuse to be faithful to him as her husband. In the story of Hosea and his wife, Gomer, we are privileged to get a glimpse of how Almighty God feels about His children when they repeatedly refuse to accept His love.

Students of the Bible debate about the holy God telling a man of God to marry someone he knew was adulterous by nature. But it reflects the reality of God and His people. God knew the character of His people when He called them in the Old Testament, and He knows the nature of the people He continues to call today. From the very beginning of humanity, God's people have been prone to unfaithfulness. From the garden on, mankind has longed for "more," has felt the urge for "other" than what God offers: the tree in the garden, the land of Egypt, meat in the wilderness, new gods in new places. Today we have our own tree, our own Egypt, our own meat, our own new gods. We, like Israel of old, continually want another choice, another resource, other indulgences and conveniences, and a selection of things to give our hearts to. History is filled with examples of God's people playing the harlot with this world. God's message to Hosea was this: feel the pain I feel. Almighty God had His heart absolutely broken by His unfaithful children. He had heaped every gift on the nation of Israel. He had freed them from bondage; He had led them to Promise; He had protected them in the presence of their enemies. He had given them a great land, made them into a great nation, and made their name great among the nations of the world. Yet despite all the love they received, God's people *would not* return His love.

From the garden on, mankind has longed for "more," has felt the urge for "other" than what God offers.

YOU CAN'T GO HOME AGAIN

Fortunately for Israel, God *is* love. Unfortunately for Israel, God also *is* justice. God's love allowed Israel to continue to exist for two hundred years even as they repeatedly and brazenly rejected His overtures. In love, the Lord waited for them to return to

Him. In love, He sent His great prophets with both the reassurance of love and the warning of certain judgment if they did not change their ways. And because He loved them, it pained Him to punish Israel for their sins. But God keeps His word. He is just and right in all He does. In the same book that so vividly reveals God's love for Israel, we read these sobering words: "Put the trumpet to your lips! An eagle is over the house of the LORD because the people have broken my covenant and rebelled against my law. . . . They sow the wind and reap the whirlwind." The people of God had enjoyed their "other" life in the nation of Israel. But they would pay for it when the whirlwind of God's judgment came down upon them.

The bird of prey that hovered over Israel was the wicked empire of Assyria. For years this greedy and cruel nation had been expanding its borders closer toward Israel. They had conquered all the land between their homeland (in the area of modern Turkey) and the home of God's delinquents. The evil empire seemed to be waiting only for God's permission to move in on His rebellious creatures, and when God removed His protection from Israel, the Assyrians swept them up and swept them away.

Assyria's practice was to remove the inhabitants from the lands they conquered, spread them over other subjugated lands, and replace them in their own land with foreigners from other vanquished countries. So the people of Israel were dispersed across the Assyrian Empire, never to return to the land God had given them. The northern kingdom of Israel was no more.

17 AND AWAY WE GO, TWO

THE SOUTHERN KINGDOM

The anger of the LORD will not turn back
until he fully accomplishes
the purposes of his heart.
In days to come
you will understand it clearly.

—JEREMIAH 23:20

1 KINGS 12–2 KINGS; 2 CHRONICLES 10–36

Does anyone ever really learn a lesson by someone else's example? Probably people who are wiser than me profit by observing other's foibles and failures. But I must be a bit obtuse, because I frequently miss other's missteps and nearly always repeat my own mistakes over and over until even I think I'm not very bright. Still, the southern kingdom of Judah seems pretty dense to have watched their relatives to the north be swept away like dandelion fluff and to have neglected to make any connection to their own situation.

Judah held on for 150 years longer than Israel did, but it wasn't because they learned anything from Israel's fate. It was because God preserved them in spite of their obliviousness. He has done the same for me more times than I can count.

BAD NEWS/GOD NEWS

The southern kingdom, made up of the two tribes of Benjamin and Judah, who had remained under the rule of Solomon's son Rehoboam, had a little something going for them that the northern kingdom of Israel did not have. Judah had God's promise that a king from David's family would always occupy the throne in Jerusalem and would rule the nation as long as it was a nation. Judah also had God's promise that the King of kings would come as a descendant of David to rule from the throne *forever*. Thus, Judah carried the seed of the coming Christ, the one who would reign over all for all time. This southern kingdom, this small nation of Judah, with so much riding on the family of David, had to survive. The fate of the entire world depended upon it.

Twenty kings reigned during the nearly 350 years the nation of Judah existed. Eight of them could have been classified as somewhat good. The standard by which the Lord rated a king of Judah was King David. That's a pretty tough standard, and as we see, not many measured up.

Judah, following the leadership of mostly bad kings, gradually drifted away from God. The first king, David's grandson Rehoboam, allowed idols to be worshiped in the nation. He wasn't quite as blatant as his counterpart in the north and may not have made idol worship the official religion of Judah, but he practiced idolatry, conducting his low worship in the high places, and the people followed his lead. God's temple, central to Jehovah worship, was located in the city of Jerusalem, and the Levites, the leaders of worship, stayed in Judah when the nation split. But in spite of those "religious advantages," Rehoboam would still establish a pattern in Judah's religion that the nation would find difficult to break.

Sometimes a good king would come along, and there would be a revival in Judah. But each good king found himself working from a pretty serious deficit that was difficult to overcome. The good king might ascend to the throne and restore the temple vessels, thus indicating that the vessels had disappeared or had been misused for probably less-than-holy practices over some stretch of time. The next good king might repair the temple or rebuild a temple gate, which obviously meant the temple had not been used and had fallen into ruin over an extended period of disuse. A king might come along and get rid of the symbols of idolatry, which meant these symbols had, over time and with some atheistic zeal, assumed God's place in the people's worship. Once, during King Hezekiah's reign, the nails were removed from the doors of the temple (meaning it had been *nailed* shut!), and the temple was cleaned out of what must have been junk. It took several Levites (I counted fourteen) a total of *sixteen days* to remove the debris that had gathered in the place. These small steps were periodically taken to try to make up ground lost during long periods of disregard for and disobedience of the Holy One of Israel. But the small steps upward never equaled the lengthy and frequent slides into the deep hole the people of Judah had dug for themselves.

Toward the dark end of Judah's slide, during King Josiah's reign, a copy of God's Law was found. It had been lost for so long that the king had never seen it or heard it read. (Actually, it is supposed that his grandfather Manasseh, perhaps the most wicked king of Judah, had destroyed every copy of the Law that could be found so he wouldn't have to know how far he was from lawful.) When Josiah heard for the first time the words of God declaring what would happen to His people because of their disobedience and idolatry, it terrified him. And well it should have. If you want to know what it is believed that he heard, read Deuteronomy 28. In these words spoken to Moses, the Lord pronounces great blessings on His people for as long as they remain faithful. But He also tells the people what will happen if they continue to disobey. Among the words used are "cursed," "plague," "horror"—and those aren't even the worst.

After Josiah heard the fearful words, a prophetess confirmed that God was indeed going to bring disaster "on this place and its people." But Josiah, because of his repentance and humility before the Lord, was given a special gift from God. He would get to die before God wreaked His vengeance on disobedient Judah. Josiah was so convicted that he led sweeping religious reforms in the nation. During his reign, for the first time in too long, the celebration of Passover was reinstituted. That means that for at least a generation the people of God had not commemorated His greatest work among them. The people had *forgotten to remember* the God who had saved them.

> *The people had forgotten to remember the God who had saved them.*

Every time something was restored in the nation of Judah, it meant that something had previously been terribly broken. But there weren't enough fixes to make up for all God's laws the people had shattered, nor would their periodic returns to God be enough to truly turn their hearts back to Him.

O Baby, It's Babylon!

During Judah's years as a nation, periodic kings and a continuous stream of bold prophets urged the people of Judah to be God's people. Isaiah and Jeremiah, among others, urged them to turn from their wicked ways so they wouldn't have to face the kind of judgment the northern tribes had faced. For brief interludes the people of Judah tried to act godly. But they couldn't seem to *be* godly, and only four years after Josiah's death, Judah once again determined that her destiny lay in the hands of idols. Twenty years after Josiah's death, Judah discovered that her destination was Babylon.

Babylon was the wonder city of the world at the end of Judah's days. It is thought to have been in the vicinity of the Garden of Eden, the cradle of the human race, and possibly near where the Tower of Babel briefly stood. Today that area is encompassed in the nation of Iraq, and you can read a description of Babylon in Isaiah 13:17–22 and Jeremiah 51:37–43 that sounds like current Iraq. But Babylon of old was the most glorious city of its time.

It was a favorite residence of kings. Assyrian kings had loved Babylon. Persian kings would occupy it in the future and revel in its pleasures. Even further in the future, Alexander the Great would bask in its glories. It was a beautiful and powerful city for centuries, reaching its peak under King Nebuchadnezzar.

On the outside Babylon was mightily fortified. Inside the city were marvels of engineering, including drawbridges, ferries, and tunnels connecting the two sides of the city, which was divided by the Euphrates River. Babylon was sometimes called "the city of gold" because it contained numerous golden images and statues. It was a religious city, with dozens of temples and more than a hundred altars to their gods. (In fact the book of Revelation speaks of "Babylon the Great" as a symbol of human efforts to build a religion and civilization without reliance on the one true God.) Nebuchadnezzar's palace was considered one of the most magnificent buildings ever erected. And of course, most lastingly famous were the Hanging Gardens, built by Nebuchadnezzar for one of his wives and noted as one of the Seven Wonders of the ancient world. The city of Babylon must have been something to behold in its day. And in its day it was the capital of the empire that ruled the world.

Nebuchadnezzar, king of Babylon, had a unique way of conquering people. He brought back to Babylon the finest men and women from the lands he conquered, and he incorporated them into the culture and functioning of his kingdom. He didn't kill them. He didn't enslave them, as we think of slavery. He had them trained to "become" Babylonian; he even changed their names to Babylonian names, as with Daniel and his three friends. And the king offered the captives the good life in the great city. This both weakened the conquered nation by taking away their best and brightest, and it strengthened his own nation with a constant influx of gifted people. That kind of treatment was hard to resist, and many of the captive people remained in Babylon by choice.

> *God would rather have His people live for a brief time in a foreign land than have them live continually like foreigners in the Promised Land.*

When the Babylonians came swooping down on the little nation of Judah as the instruments of God's judgment, the people of Judah would have had a hard time seeing that anything good would ever come from Nebuchadnezzar's conquering Jerusalem. His army surrounded the city, cutting them off from the outside and forcing terrible famine and degradation upon the citizens. When he finally took the city, he burned down the temple and destroyed the city walls.

Nebuchadnezzar deported the people of Judah to Babylon in stages. In the first deportation, he took the choice people in the land, which included the wondrous Daniel and three young men who would prove themselves as God's servants in Nebuchadnezzar's fire. The second group taken to Babylon was probably the skilled people and artisans, and the third deportation took all but the poorest and most "useless" to Babylon. Altogether, seventy thousand of God's little captives arrived in Babylon, and in that foreign land they remained for seventy years.

In addition to the people of Judah, Nebuchadnezzar also captured the articles of the temple. God's treasury would be used to serve a lesser god than Jehovah, and God's people would be used to serve a lesser king than He. But God would rather have His people live for a brief time in a foreign land than have them live continually *like foreigners* in the Promised Land. So God would use His people's captivity in Babylon like Nebuchadnezzar's fire on Shadrach, Meshach, and Abednego—as a crucible to purge idolatry from the lives and the hearts of His people. And when He brought His people back, they would once more and forever be His.

KINGDOMS COME

When the youthful Daniel was taken captive along with the best of Judah, he resolved not to fit the Babylonian model. In fact, only Daniel maintained his Hebrew name; even his three friends became known to us by their Babylonian names. Daniel faced the same choice most of us as children of God will face: when we're out of our element, when we're out of our country, when we're out from under the authority that governs our behavior, what will we be? How will we behave? Will we uphold the standards that we have given lip service to? Daniel, through many years of close association with the king of Babylon, would be a good friend to the megalomaniacal monarch, but Daniel would in every way remain an ally of the Lord God. He was rather like Abraham. He had to leave everything he knew and had previously depended upon and go to a land that would be shown him by God. Once there, he would find out why he was there. Through Daniel, God would reveal to Nebuchadnezzar, and to us, how He was going to save not just the people of Judah but all the people of the world.

Daniel faced the same choice most of us as children of God will face: when we're out of our element, will we uphold the standards that we have given lip service to?

It all started with a strange dream. In fact, the book of Daniel is filled with strange dreams and visions. Some of his visions we recognize as already being fulfilled in past events. Some of them . . . well I leave them for other people to explain. Confusing as they are, each of the visions points to one thing: the sovereignty of God. The Lord God Almighty is in charge of all things, and everything that has happened, is happening, and will happen is under His dominion.

One night Nebuchadnezzar had a dream that greatly troubled him. As dreams were considered to be messages from the gods, the king sent for the people he believed could tell him what the dream *was* and what it *meant.* But his stable of magicians, sorcerers, and astrologers couldn't tell him what he had dreamed, so they certainly couldn't tell him what it meant. Daniel went to God to solve the mystery and then went to Nebuchadnezzar with God's interpretation of his mysterious dream. And in telling the king of Babylon about his future, the King of the universe told about the future of all people to come. The dream portrayed that earthly kingdoms would come and go, and yet in the midst of earthly kingdoms, God's kingdom, a kingdom sovereign and eternal, would be established.

Nebuchadnezzar had dreamed of "an enormous, dazzling statue, awesome in appearance." The statue had a head of pure gold, a chest and arms of silver, a belly and thighs of bronze, legs of iron, and feet of iron mixed with baked clay. As he watched the statue, a rock was cut out of stone and not by human hands. The rock struck the statue on its feet and smashed them. The iron, the clay, the bronze, the silver, and the gold were broken to pieces at the same time and became like dust, which was swept away by the wind, leaving no trace of the statue. Then the rock that had struck the statue became a huge mountain and filled the whole earth.

We know, because of what has happened in history, what the dream meant. At the time, though, it was a stunningly accurate portrayal of what would happen in the future. The head of gold represented the Babylonian Empire and its dominion over the world of its time. After Babylon would come an "inferior" kingdom, represented by the inferior metal silver. And after that, a third kingdom would rule over the whole earth. Finally there would come a fourth kingdom, strong as iron, which breaks and crushes all other things. But this kingdom would be partly strong and partly brittle, as represented by the mix of iron and baked clay. And then these words follow the explanation of the statue: "In the time of those kings [the strong yet brittle kingdom], the God of heaven will set up a kingdom that will never be destroyed, nor will it be left to another people. It will crush all those kingdoms and bring them to an end, but it will itself endure forever." Babylon was eventually overcome by the "inferior" Persian Empire, which was defeated by the Greeks, who were consumed into the powerful Roman Empire. And during the days of Roman occupation of the known world, Jesus Christ was born King of kings forever and ever . . .

God Knew Good News

Through Daniel, God revealed what would happen. And it happened just as God had said. It happened for the good of God's people. And it happened for the good of humanity.

Some time later during Daniel's life in Babylon, Nebuchadnezzar died and was replaced by kings who could not match his achievements. These kings gradually squandered the greatness of Babylon and were replaced by the Persian ruler Cyrus the Great, who virtually just stepped into power there. He took over what was already running fairly well, and part of the running was done by Daniel. The Persian ruler, recognizing that Daniel, now an old man, was still a great asset, kept him on as an adviser and administrator. The Persians retained control of the former Babylonian Empire and eventually allowed the people of Judah to return home. Quite different from the Assyrians or the Babylonians, Cyrus the Great encouraged exiles to go back to their homelands. Do you think it was all Cyrus's doing?

A milestone was about to be reached in the lives of God's people: they were approaching their seventieth year in captivity. So? Well, God had previously told the people that he would limit their time in captivity, and then . . . then He had plans for them. "'When seventy years are completed for Babylon, I will come to you and fulfill my gracious promise to bring you back to this place. For I know the plans I have for you,' declares the LORD, 'plans to prosper you and not to harm you, plans to give you hope and a future. Then you will call upon me and come and pray to me, and I will listen to you. You will seek me and find me when you seek me with all your heart. I will be found by you,' declares the LORD, 'and will bring you back from captivity. I will gather you from all the nations and places where I have banished you,' declares the LORD, 'and will bring you back to the place from which I carried you into exile.'"

God still had much to accomplish through His people. He had *plans* for them.

God had once placed His holy nation of Israel at the crossroads of the world, with trade routes running north to south and east to west. The location had been a magnet for invaders who wanted to control the land. It had also facilitated David's expansion of Israel's borders and Solomon's increase in its riches. But I don't think that is why they were placed at the crossroads. I believe God's people were placed there because their job was to *influence a world for God.* They hadn't done a great job the first time, choosing instead to let the world influence them. They had adopted the gods and the ways of the pagan cultures around them. And because they had refused to fulfill God's purpose, God had swept them away.

But they were different people now. They had been humbled. Would they allow God to use them to work out His plan for the entire world?

YOU *CAN* GO HOME AGAIN

During the years of captivity in Babylon, some pretty significant things happened. The people of God finally lost their desire for other gods. Was it the punishment brought on them by God, or the acceptance of their own sinfulness, or the ultimate recognition that their false gods had done nothing for them? Whatever it had taken to purge their urge for idols, they now embraced Jehovah God. They had also begun to worship and study in a new format since they had lost access to the temple, but their study was of the Holy God, and their worship was to Him only. The captive people had formed synagogues, which meant "gatherings," and they gathered with regularity and worshiped and studied with a zeal that had been missing from their corporate worship for generations. Even after the temple was rebuilt by Herod the Great, the Jews (now so called because they were from Ju-dah?) still met in the synagogues, and since Christ honored their choice, it must have been right with God. God's people, at the end of captivity, were trying to find God and live like God wanted them to live. He would honor both desires.

Three groups of captives had been taken from Judah to Babylon. The people would return to their land in a similar way.

Cyrus the Great, "in order to fulfill the word of the LORD spoken by Jeremiah," allowed those who wanted to, to return to their homeland and rebuild the temple, which had been destroyed by Nebuchadnezzar. Many were moved to go back home—more than forty thousand, in fact. (Of course, reflecting the nature of humans everywhere, more decided to stay in Babylon, where they had an easy and profitable life and could avoid the danger and deprivation of a long trip and a hard job.) After taking up a collection to finance the journey, the first group returned to Jerusalem, led by Zerubbabel, a descendant of David. They carried the temple vessels (probably turned over to them by Cyrus as a goodwill gesture) and made a four-month journey back to their homeland with the purpose of rebuilding the temple. It was an arduous trip and a difficult task. There was trouble and discouragement, but with the help of rallying words spoken by the prophets Haggai and Zechariah, the task was eventually completed, and the new temple was dedicated. Then the people celebrated Passover. The observation of Passover always seems appropriate after God has delivered in yet another way.

Nearly sixty years after completing the new temple, during the reign of the Persian king Artaxerxes, a priest named Ezra led a second, smaller group back to Jerusalem. He was a descendant of Aaron and was a "teacher well versed in the Law of Moses." Now that the temple was rebuilt, Ezra's task was to rebuild the people, many of whom had already fallen into bad ways after mingling with those who had inhabited their land during the Jews' exile. Ezra led the people in a spiritual revival, taught a new generation the Law, and instituted synagogue services in the new/old land.

The final major group to return was led by Nehemiah, cupbearer to King Artaxerxes. He had an important job in Babylon, but when he heard from some travelers that things weren't going well in his homeland because the walls of Jerusalem were broken down and the gates had been burned, he asked for a leave of absence to see what he could do to remedy the situation. In spite of the fatigue from a grueling journey, continuous opposition from foes in the land, and crippling discouragement among the workers, Nehemiah accomplished the task in less than two months! With all the technology and tools we have today, with the kind of work force we could muster, imagine what could be done if we took on that task now. Why, we could probably do it in two years!

RETURNED TO SENDER

And so the people of God were in the Promised Land once more. They had returned to God and returned to the land from which they had been exiled because of their disobedience, their disbelief.

The entire Old Testament is a tribute to just how much God has loved His people. As the story is truly told and foretold in the Old book, so it will be fulfilled in the New.

As the Old Testament historical account closes, God's people are being rebuilt both physically and spiritually. God sent His people into captivity to teach them to obey. He saved them in captivity to teach them to trust. And then, to teach them of His incredible love, He brought them back home just as He had promised that He would. God saved His people because He had a plan for them. He had always had a plan. The New Testament will open as once again God begins to reveal to His people just what His plan has *always* been about.

The final book in the Old Testament, Malachi, is one of seventeen books of prophecy calling God's people to return to Him, and it opens with these words: "I have loved you," says the LORD. "But you ask, '*How* have you loved us?'" How has God loved? Let me count the ways! The entire Old Testament is a tribute to just how *much* God has loved His people, and the whole of the testimonial has enumerated just *how* He has loved. As the story of God's astonishing and awesome love is truly told and foretold in the Old book, so it will be fulfilled in the New.

18 THIS MUST BE LOVE

THE KING COMES

In the beginning was the Word, and the Word was with God,
and the Word was God. . . . The Word became flesh
and made his dwelling among us.
We have seen his glory, the glory of the One and Only,
who came from the Father, full of grace and truth.

—JOHN 1:1, 14

I know I've been hard on God's chosen people of old (I actually kind of specialize in being hard on God's people of any time, including myself), but I am continually floored by how faithless His people are while He is always so faithful to them. I'm sure my expectations are a little, to use an earlier expression, too lofty regarding how God's people *should* act. Still, God's chosen people, the Israelites—the Jews as the New Testament opens—had such a storied past with the Holy One of Israel. They had such an intimate experience with God and His promises to them. They should have understood, right?

It would be incredibly reassuring to turn the page in God's Book and find out that His chosen people had finally and for all time figured out why they had been chosen, what their God was all about and what all it meant for them to belong to Him. I would love to read the page that confirms God's exiles returned home, rebuilt their city, rebuilt their temple, rebuilt their lives, and built an incredible faith in the

God who had saved them from their enemies and from their exile and had promised to save them from their sins. What a page that would be!

I wish I could say this is finally the page. But I can't, and it isn't.

KEEPING THE FAITH

When we turn the page from the Old Testament to the New Testament, we turn the page on four hundred years. The people of God are still in the Promised Land. That's the good news. The bad news is that the promise is looking a little dim to them. And *their* land? Well, it doesn't really belong to them at the moment.

In those four hundred years the world had seen several changes in regimes. The Medo-Persian Empire, in power when God's people had returned to their land, had endured some raging battles with the Greeks (check out any number of Hollywood movies or watch the History Channel for information). The Greeks, under the leadership of the young Alexander the Great, finally overthrew the Persians, and for quite some time Greece ruled the world in some semblance of peace. However, out west an empire was rising in Rome, iron tough and determined to rule the world in Greece's place. (Nebuchadnezzar's statue dream isn't doing badly so far.) Sixty years or so before the opening of the New Testament period, the Romans conquered the world, including the land where God's people waited. The little settlement of Jews and the mighty Romans who tried to cohabit with them had developed a fractious relationship. The Promised Land was a cauldron of resentment, including a fair share of resentment toward God.

For four hundred years the people had not heard one new word from God. Not one prophet had appeared; not one promise had been fulfilled. Well, forgive them all to pieces, but didn't they have the right to be a little bit perturbed? God had told them He would be with them, but apparently He had forgotten where they were. They were in their land, sure, but it was crowded with foreigners and foreign ways. Their nation even had a foreign name now: "Palestine," after their old nemesis, the Philistines, as if those barbarians had prior claim to Israel's Promised Land. The present natives of the land also spoke a foreign language. Hebrew was just the language of the Law now. The regular people spoke Aramaic, which they had learned during captivity, and they (and nearly everyone else in the whole world) understood a bit of Greek from the days when yet another group had control over things. And at least one other thing felt foreign. They could get out of their country and travel all over the world on roads and across bridges built by the Romans, but they still felt like prisoners in their own land because of the Roman occupation. Didn't they have a reason for being a little uncertain about God's remembering them?

Did God remember? Was He going to keep His word?

Even though it appeared to God's people that He had been doing nothing in the last four hundred years and had forgotten what He had promised, He had been quite busy, not only in the affairs of His own people, but in the affairs of the rest of the world. He had been planning for His Word to go on and then go out. Four hundred years He spent preparing the way—nearly everything that God's people considered wrong about their world, God had manufactured, and He was going to make it right for sending His Word into the whole world. When His Word finally went out from His people, it would travel across the world on roads and bridges built by Rome and across land and sea protected by the might of the Roman army and the laws of safe passage they enforced. When God's Word went out across the world, it would be universally understood, because the world had a working knowledge of the Greek language, thanks to Alexander the Great and his Greeks. Someday God's Word would explode across the world. Thank you, Greece. Thank you, Rome. And *all* thanks be to God Almighty, who always had a plan. God's Word would be spoken for all to hear when the time was right. And, as the New Testament pages open, the time was right.

God was ready to speak His Word.

WHISPERING HOPE

It all started with whispers. Angel whispers. Old priest Zechariah heard them. He heard that he and his wife, Elizabeth, would bear a son in their old age, a son who would go before the Lord and prepare the way and make God's people ready to receive Him.

Young Mary heard the whisper. She heard that she would carry the Seed in her body and that she would give birth to the Son of the Most High God.

Mary's betrothed, Joseph, heard the whisper. He heard that Holy God was *in* Mary.

If God's people, who were waiting for God to act, had only been listening . . . They might have heard the whispers, or they might have heard the song some lowly shepherds heard one dark night. They might have heard the heavens split open and an angel chorus burst forth, declaring the birth of the King.

If God's people, who were waiting for God to act, had only been looking . . .

They might have seen what some wiser men saw in the eastern sky. Have you ever wondered how stargazers from far away could follow a star for miles and months and yet no one else in the whole village noticed its glow? It had to be a pretty special star if the wise men recognized it as "his star." But the Jews, God's chosen? They missed it. I guess that's what happens if you get so dismayed with the bad goings-on around you that you forget to look up! Still, how did the people nearby miss seeing some really well-dressed men (at least in all the pageants they look pretty fancy) carrying very expensive gifts to a child in the neighborhood? Shouldn't they have noticed at least that?

When we have a preconceived idea of what God should be doing for our sake, we frequently miss what He is doing for our good.

In spite of all the whispers, God's waiting people never heard. In spite of all the signs, God's waiting people never saw. They were so sure what God *should* do for them that they totally missed what He *did* do for them. What a lesson for us. When we have a preconceived idea of what God should be doing for our *sake,* we frequently miss what He is doing for our *good.*

For the good of His people then, God acted. For the good of His people then, God spoke. And for the good of His people now and forever, He still acts and He still speaks . . . and it is still the same Word.

IN A WORD . . .

When all the world was right for God's Word to spread across the world, God spoke His Word. He who had spoken the world into existence spoke the Word who would save the world, a world that had gone so wrong: wrong again, wrong still, wrong always. But the Word God spoke was missed because it wasn't the word people were expecting.

When God's Word became flesh in Jesus Christ, He entered a world that wanted something "else." And consequently, though the whole world was prepared, the *hearts* of God's people were not. His people didn't accept who He was because they wanted so much "more." They wanted the Lion of Judah to slay their enemies. He would, instead, be the Lamb of God who would die for His enemies. They wanted a fighter. He would be a healer. They would demand He rule. He would require they serve.

All prophecy forgotten or misunderstood, the people of God refused to see anything of God in God's Chosen One: Jesus the Christ. One more time, in a long history of times, God's people decided to go in another direction than the way God led. And, warning us once more, they really believed they were right in what they did.

Jesus of Nazareth, of questionable parentage, was a good man, but He was a poor Messiah. He mounted a platform instead of a horse, and he used sharp words rather than a sword. In the chosen ones' eyes, Jesus just couldn't be who He claimed to be. And though the wounded and the weary people flocked to hear His words and be healed by His hands, the "religious" people just knew that what Jesus said and what Jesus did wasn't "right." Though Jesus served, He never ruled, and that certainly wasn't right for the self-righteous and the religious and the political. By their interpretation of their own law, they were within their rights when they decided to get rid of this Messiah who was so wrong by their standards.

God's people decided to kill God's Messenger. And they did. They orchestrated the death of the One who came *to* them, the One who came *from* them, the One who came *for* them.

But the Message got through anyway. There were people who had heard the whispers. And there were people who had marveled at the words spoken by the Messenger. There were people who had seen the signs and who recognized the fulfillment of prophecy in the One who came. There were followers. There were believers who would take the word of God's coming and the Word of God's salvation, and they would spread it across the world. The message would be in Greek for the world to understand, and the message would spread to the world along roads that Rome had built. And the Word would live. And the Word would change the *hearts* of mankind, which was all God had ever wanted anyway: people with a *heart for Him.*

God chose once. Now the choice is ours. We get to choose what we believe. We get to choose whom we believe. We can choose God's way, or we can choose our own. We can accept His gift, or we can long for more or better or just different. We can sleep through His coming, or we can watch for His coming back. We can give up in hopelessness, believing that things will never turn around, or we can live in the hopeful expectation that the One who made all things right in the beginning can once more make things right for all time. The choice is ours, and as it was in the beginning and now and ever shall be, it *all* hinges on the choice we make.

> He came to that which was his own,
> but his own did not receive him.
> Yet to all who received him,
> to those who believed in his name,
> he gave the right to become children of God.

—JOHN 1:11–12

. . . LOVE

The Holy Bible tells a story. It's a long story. It's one story. It all began in the heart of the Creator. It unfolds as God gives His heart, gives His plan, gives His Word, and gives His life in the hope that the created one will give himself back to the God who created him for just such a purpose.

From the very beginning, God's plan was in place. *Only* love could have thought it up. *Only* love could have carried it out. *Only* love could have endured the sinful desires of mankind and determined to save him anyway. This must be love: to save a creature who proves himself in every way undeserving of salvation.

Love was begun in a garden . . . revealed in a manger . . . fulfilled on a cross.

Love extends even to those who won't acknowledge Him today.

Love reaches all the way . . . even to you and me.

We read one story throughout. But what a story! A story of *amazing* love.

My prayer is that you have discovered *you* are amazingly loved.

ENDNOTES

CHAPTER 1

"Where can I go from your Spirit?"—Psalm 139:7–10

"The eyes of the Lord are everywhere"—Proverbs 15:3

"Can anyone hide in secret places"—Jeremiah 23:24

"nothing in all creation is hidden from God's sight"—Hebrews 4:13

where light lives, where the oceans begin—Job 38

"He who forms the hearts"—Psalm 33:15

"God knows your hearts"—Luke 16:15

"Ah, Sovereign Lord, you have made the heavens"—Jeremiah 32:17

"To whom, then, will you compare God?"—Isaiah 40:18, 22

"The Lord has established his throne in heaven"—Psalm 103:19

"For the Lord is the great God"—Psalm 95:3–6

all law is summed up in love—See Matthew 22:34–40.

the greatest thing is love—See 1 Corinthians 13.

CHAPTER 2

"In the beginning God"—Genesis 1:1

"I AM"—Exodus 3:14

"In the beginning God created"—Genesis 1:1

"Now the earth was formless"—Genesis 1:2

"And the Spirit of God was hovering"—Genesis 1:2

"The heavens declare the glory of God"—Psalm 19:1

"For since the creation of the world"—Romans 1:20

"Let there be light"—Genesis 1:3

"fixed limits for it"—Job 38:8–11

"He himself gives all men life"—Acts 17:25

"Very good"—Genesis 1:31

CHAPTER 3

spoke things into existence—Genesis 1:3, 6, 14, 20, 24, 26, 28

"You are free to eat"—Genesis 2:16–17

"For God so loved"—John 3:16

"man after [God's] own heart"—1 Samuel 13:14

"masquerades as an angel of light"—2 Corinthians 11:14

"model of perfection"—Ezekiel 28:12

"anointed," "ordained," "walked among"—Ezekiel 28:14

"wickedness was found"—Ezekiel 28:15

"There is a way that seems right"—Proverbs 14:12

CHAPTER 4

"Where are you?"—Genesis 3:9

"Where is your brother?"—Genesis 4:9

"the sons of God saw"—Genesis 6:2

Enoch and his son Methuselah—Genesis 5:21–27

"walked with God"—Genesis 5:22

"grieved," "his heart was filled with pain"—Genesis 6:6

"wipe mankind"—Genesis 6:7

"but Noah found favor"—Genesis 6:8

Adam had named the animals—Genesis 2:19–20

lived in vegetarian peace—Genesis 1:29–30

dog-eat-dog world—Genesis 9:2–3

government would have authority to shed blood—Genesis 9:5–6

every inclination of man's heart—Genesis 8:21

"Whenever I bring clouds"—Genesis 9:14–16

"Come, let us build ourselves a city"—Genesis 11:4

"came down"—Genesis 11:5

"confused"—Genesis 11:9

CHAPTER 5

out of idolatry—Joshua 24:2

"announced the gospel"—Galatians 3:8

"My covenant in your flesh"—Genesis 17:13

"Take your son"—Genesis 22:2

"Stay here"—Genesis 22:5

"God himself will provide"—Genesis 22:8

account of Abraham's faith—Hebrews 11:8–19

"But we never can prove"—John H. Sammis, "Trust and Obey," 1887.

CHAPTER 6

"wild donkey of a man"—Genesis 16:12

"before he had finished praying"—Genesis 24:15

"As soon as he had seen the nose ring"—Genesis 24:30

prophecy concerning the children—Genesis 25:19–23

didn't choose the younger because he deserved it—Romans 9:11–12

"whole body like a hairy garment"—Genesis 25:25

"despised" his birthright—Genesis 25:34

"consoling himself with the thought of killing"—Genesis 27:42

he dreamed of a stairway—Genesis 28:10–15

"Surely the LORD is in this place"—Genesis 28:16

"lovely in form"—Genesis 29:17

"weak eyes"—Genesis 29:17

"Oh what a tangled web"—Sir Walter Scott, *Marmion,* canto 6, stanza 17.

"When the LORD saw that Leah was not loved"—Genesis 29:31

Leah "hired" Jacob—Genesis 30:16

leaned on the top of his staff—Hebrews 11:21

CHAPTER 7

"richly ornamented robe"—Genesis 37:3

"Now Israel loved Joseph"—Genesis 37:3

"hated him"—Genesis 37:4

"When his brothers saw"—Genesis 37:4

"they hated him all the more"—Genesis 37:8

"kept the matter in mind"—Genesis 37:11

"pondered . . . in her heart"—Luke 2:19

"the LORD was with [Joseph]"—Genesis 39:2, 3, 21, 23

"by a great deliverance"—Genesis 45:7

"intended it for good"—Genesis 50:20

"Know for certain"—Genesis 15:13–14

"I am God"—Genesis 46:3–4

CHAPTER 8

"a new king, who did not know about Joseph"—Exodus 1:8

"fine child"—Exodus 2:2

Moses left behind the temporary reward—Hebrews 11:24–25

"Who am I?"—Exodus 3:11

"Suppose I go to the Israelites"—Exodus 3:13

"I AM WHO I AM"—Exodus 3:14

"I AM has sent me to you"—Exodus 3:14

"This is my name forever"—Exodus 3:15

Jesus and Martha at Lazarus's grave—John 11:11–45

CHAPTER 9

"Do not be afraid"—Exodus 14:13–14

The Lord is fighting for them—See Exodus 14:25.

"And when the Israelites saw"—Exodus 14:31

"I will completely blot out"—Exodus 17:14

"You yourselves have seen"—Exodus 19:4–6

"do everything the LORD has said"—Exodus 19:8

613 laws—"Mitzvot: The Commandments," Religion Facts, www.religionfacts.com/judaism/practices/mitzvot.htm

the law as a schoolmaster—Galatians 3:24, KJV

"this fellow Moses"—Exodus 32:1

"your people"—Exodus 32:7

"the sound of war"—Exodus 32:17

"Show me your glory"—Exodus 33:18

"goodness"—Exodus 33:19

"back" of God—Exodus 33:23

CHAPTER 10

flames consumed the outskirts—See Numbers 11:1.

"It was the season for the first ripe grapes"—Numbers 13:20

"We should go up and take possession"—Numbers 13:30

"We can't . . . they are stronger"—Numbers 13:31

"wholeheartedly"—Numbers 14:24

"Listen, you rebels"—Numbers 20:10

"Only be careful"—Deuteronomy 4:9

"When you have eaten and are satisfied"—Deuteronomy 8:10–18

"his eyes were not weak nor his strength gone"—Deuteronomy 34:7

CHAPTER 11

"No prophet has risen in Israel"—Deuteronomy 34:10–12

"to go out and come in before them"—Numbers 27:17

Solomon's palace took thirteen years—1 Kings
7:1
"held fast to them in love"—1 Kings 11:2
"certainly" tear the kingdom—1 Kings 11:11
"for the sake of David"—1 Kings 11:12

CHAPTER 16
"no one can serve two masters"—Matthew 6:24
"from the LORD"—1 Kings 12:15
the Lord's "doing"—1 Kings 12:22–24
"Here are your gods, O Israel"—1 Kings 12:28
"caused Israel to sin"—1 Kings 22:52; 2 Kings
23:15
"You have done more evil"—1 Kings 14:9
"He not only considered it trivial"—1 Kings
16:31–33
"Put the trumpet to your lips!"—Hosea 8:1, 7

CHAPTER 17
"on this place and its people"—2 Chronicles
34:24
"Babylon the Great"—Revelation 14–18
"an enormous, dazzling statue, awesome in
appearance"—Daniel 2:31
"In the time of those kings"—Daniel 2:44
"When seventy years are completed"—Jeremiah
29:10–14
"in order to fulfill the word"—Ezra 1:1
"teacher well versed"—Ezra 7:6
"I have loved you"—Malachi 1:2

CHAPTER 18
"his star"—Matthew 2:2